Blossom!

*It's Not What Life Throws At You...
It's How You Catch It.*

Nancy Proud Freebery
Illustrations by Pat Macht Bulat

Blossom!
It's Not What Life Throws At You...It's How You Catch It

FIRST EDITION

Copyright © 2002 by Nancy Proud Freebery

All rights reserved.
Not to be reproduced in whole or in part in any form
without written permission from the publisher, except by
a reviewer who may quote brief passages in a review.

ISBN # 0–9715656–8-6

Library of Congress Control Number: 2001119941

Published by
NPF Communications
Newark, Delaware
www.npfcommunications.com
(More contact information last page)

Printed in the United States of America
by Modern Press, Wilmington, Delaware

Cover design and layout by Wendy J. Wheeler

*With love and gratitude
this book is dedicated to
my husband, Rick
our son, Ricky
and
my parents, Jane and Charles Proud*

CONTENTS

Acknowledgements	*vii*
Preface	1
Chapter 1 - Struggle	
Ricky's Story	7
My Business Challenge	23
Strained Relationships	28
Accumulated Stress	32
My Revelation	41
Chapter 2 - Understanding	
What IS With Ricky?	45
The Mind, Body & Soul Connection	57
Chapter 3 - Action	
What To Do About Ricky?	63
What To Do About Me?	71
Spirit to the Rescue	74
Mental Fitness	76
Relationships	83
Work	86
Nutrition	87
Exercise	92
Rest	96
Let the Good Cycle Begin!	99
Chapter 4 - Acceptance	105
Chapter 5 - Living Wholly	119
Afterword	129
Resources	133

ACKNOWLEDGEMENTS

My sincere thanks to the following people for helping me make this book a reality. First to the "crew" who graciously took time from their busy schedules to read the draft manuscript and give me helpful feedback – my husband, Rick; my son, Ricky; my sister, Christine Bubley; my parents, Jane and Charles Proud; Sharon Albrecht, S. Charles Bean, M.D.; Dee Bruni, Laura Carpenter, Kathy Carruthers, Cinda Cattermole, Elaine (Pip) Concklin, Kathryn Harris, LCSW; Wendy Harron, OTR/L; Bernadette Hearn, Kate Lorenz, Susan McPheeters, and Barbara Russo.

Special thanks to Lynn Carpenter, Kathy Craven and Coo Murray for reading the final manuscript and offering me the encouragement I needed to complete the task!

Gratitude galore to artist Pat Macht Bulat for her amazing ability to take from my mind the vision for the *Blossom!* icon and bring it to life in such an inspired way.

The list would not be complete without special recognition to Ralph Trushell and his team at Modern Press. Ralph and I go way back professionally and it helped so much to be able to work with a familiar group to print this book. Thanks especially to Wendy J. Wheeler for her patience and skill in making my wishes come true for the cover design and layout.

Way to go, everybody!

PREFACE

I was blessed with one opportunity to be a mother. This book is about how I have grown from the struggles of parenting my neurologically impaired son.

It started as a book that I wished someone had given me at the beginning of my journey. I needed a message of hope and inspiration. It seemed like life was going to be a real struggle, and it has been. But if I had known that tucked along the path would be a life lesson in wholeness that would make my life more meaningful than would have been possible without the struggle, I would have been more encouraged. I would have been looking. As it was, I took off down the path with fear and worry as my companions and I learned as I went.

This book is about what I learned. I do not have any secret cure for life's struggles, just a story with some lessons meant to help make life more hopeful for others.

I discovered that it's not what life throws at you, it's how you catch it that makes the difference. We all struggle at some point along the way. This book is about keeping your chin up so you can catch what's thrown your way and use it to help you grow. The title *Blossom!* and the radiant, filled-with-life flower on the cover represent nature's transformation - the promise of growth

PREFACE

and hope. This book is about my transformation and that of my son. It is about human potential and the absolute connection between the mind, body, soul and spirit. It is meant to comfort. I hope it will inspire.

I have you walk with me along my path, so you can see where I was and and how I grew. It was a process. It began with understanding. I learned that once you truly understand your struggle, everything else falls into place. Understanding paved the way to action where I found that there really was not going to be a "quick fix." I introduce you to seven ingredients that helped me improve my personal well being and my ability to rise above the stresses of of my struggle. I learned how to go with the flow, to live now, to be patient, and to balance my life – pretty potent lessons for anybody! From there I uncovered the freedom of acceptance. No more trying to fight my son's disability, control it, or make it go away. Once I learned to accept it, an unexpected, transforming growth slowly unfolded like the petals of a newly opening blossom! I realized that along the way, I had been given the gifts of wisdom, grace, tolerance, compassion, and thankfulness – gifts that reveal a depth and wholeness only to those who struggle.

PREFACE

There is so much life to be lived between the struggle and the "it's all better." Please don't wait for the "it's all better" because it may never be. But that's okay – you can live now, healthfully and wholly. What starts out to be the most difficult time of your life can become the most fulfilling lesson of your life. Come walk with me down my path…keep your eyes open.

Let's start at the beginning.

struggle

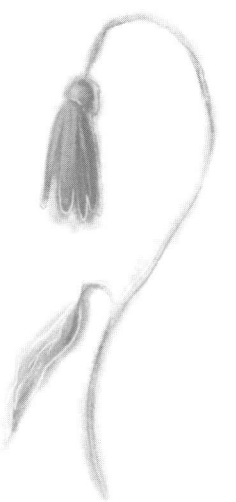

Rick and I had been married for five years when Ricky was born. I was thirty-one and Rick was thirty-seven. After several years of "working through" infertility, we miraculously conceived on our own. No drugs, no surgical procedures...just a gift from above. Hallelujah!

Ricky came into the world on a perfect day. It was so uncharacteristically humidity-free for July in Delaware that we still talk about it. It was a special day for our special child. We so wanted to have children, prayed for children, worked hard – as anyone who has been through infertility can attest – for our precious child. We loved this boy with every ounce of love we had – and still do. BUT, parenting was not easy for us. It was a struggle.

Ricky was born almost a month early. I developed high blood pressure when I went into early labor and he had to be delivered. That should have been our first warning. Instead, we thought no problem, we'll just have our baby and carry on. I delivered him naturally. He weighed five pounds and everything checked out at birth. He was tiny. I called him my peanut. I began to breast feed and to my surprise they sent us home from the hospital on time. Oh no!

CHAPTER 1 – STRUGGLE

He was loved, coddled, and had all the attention a child should have. I had resigned from my ten-year career as a marketing communications professional, hoping to have a month off to prepare for motherhood. Premature delivery took care of that! Rick and I had decided that I would stay home with our child, at least for the first three years. We felt very fortunate that we could make this decision.

Well, ten years of fifty-hour professional work weeks did not prepare me for what was to come! Poor Ricky was flat out unsettled. He cried all the time! First we thought it was because his nights and days were mixed – although he really didn't sleep anyway. Then we thought his digestive system just wasn't fully "ripe." Then we decided it was ME, of course. I was too fired-up, my nerves were messing up my milk, I needed to be more relaxed…I needed to get back to exercising…me, me, me. It was all my fault. This diagnosis persisted…at least in my mind!

We tried everything – I adjusted my diet in hopes of helping my breast milk. I tried, without success, to get back to working out. I was just plum tuckered out. Sleep deprivation took its toll! We gave Ricky prescription stomach settling drops. I rocked, massaged, sang, talked, pleaded, cried. The poor little fella would just wail, I mean like the sound of a cat…you know that high-pitched wail? And he just could not stop!

Rick was the first to become discouraged. He concluded that no couple in their right minds would have more than one child if this were normal. I kept the faith, thinking "it's what babies do…he'll grow out of it." I had to. This was my new chosen profession – twenty-four hours a day, seven days a week. If I threw in the towel, oh what a mess it would be. I'm not saying I was a saint. I felt isolated, stressed, low, and exhausted to the point where my head always ached and my body literally throbbed. But I never recall realizing at the time how difficult the situation was. I just went on. Days and nights blended into one another. I was able to bond with love, and fully care for Ricky. I really wanted him to settle in and stop crying. I know I gave him my very, very best. I now know how fortunate we were that I was able to give him good, loving care.

As a baby, Ricky was very often sick. Never anything serious. Upper respiratory infections which would lead to never-ending ear infections. Terrifying croup attacks, gastrointestinal troubles, which, when reoccurring in an infant, raised concerns. Loads of liquids and bottom balm…poor fella – he sure had a time. I questioned the pediatrician about the normalcy of all this unsettledness and ill health and was assured it was just Ricky…really nothing over which to be greatly concerned. I was constantly telling Rick how fortunate we were that I did not have to work. We seemed to be at the doctor's office every ten days. On antibiotics, off antibiotics, get well, get sick, develop allergies to the antibiotics…so many mothers know the drill. Any boss in his right mind would have had to call me down for too much missed time. I was so lucky, at least I didn't have to deal with that! I sympathize with those of you who do when your child is frequently ill.

Ricky grew, gained weight – though not much – and reached most infant milestones within the appropriate time. Although he never slept for very long, by the age of three he finally did sleep through the night, but he always woke at the literal crack of dawn – and still does – more than ready to GO! His continuous crying subsided, but he was still unusually unsettled. He screamed bloody murder when I would try to have his hair cut. Stroller rides always ended with me carrying him back, crying, while I pushed the stroller…pretty much feeling defeated that I couldn't do something to comfort my child.

Ricky's temperament was a weird thing. Since I spent so much time with him, I was convinced that his difficult behavior was not intentional. His core spirit was that of a very sweet, loving little boy. When he was settled, there was a kindness about him. It was just something I could feel. Since Rick mostly experienced Ricky's unsettled behavior, it was often hard to convince him that it did not seem intentional. Parental strain over Ricky was, and still is, an ongoing family issue.

When Ricky was three, we enrolled him in preschool, just a couple of days a week for a couple of hours a day. Over time, I noticed my usually unsettled, active little guy became very quiet and reserved as I would walk him to his classroom. After several months, one of his more abrupt preschool teachers asked me, "What's with Ricky…can he hear okay?" Well, needless to say I was concerned and hurt. She said this very matter of factly and within earshot of the other mothers in the hall. My first concern, of course, was – could he hear? He had so many ear infections that perhaps his hearing was

CHAPTER 1 STRUGGLE

damaged. We visited the pediatrician and he administered a hearing test. Ricky could hear just fine. Now I felt uneasy about Ricky and preschool. Up until now, I just thought we had an unsettled child. Ricky's preschool experience was now, unfortunately, making me anxious. It wasn't much fun.

During this first preschool year, I could see that his projects looked different from all of the other children's work. Theirs looked like the intended objects and Ricky's work was more like a blur. I observed that he was definitely more imaginative than most of his peers. Pretend play made up a good 95% of his play. He was kind, and shared without the usual "it's MINE" issues that most children his age exhibit. He seemed pretty smart for his age. When his first preschool year concluded, the report showed that he was a sweet boy, but the teachers noted that his motor skills and attention span needed improvement.

The preschool director called me at home and suggested Ricky be evaluated by an outside group. She really thought his motor skills could use extra work. She mentioned occupational therapy and I thought, "Geez, I don't think he plans to get a job for years!" I obviously did not understand occupational therapy. She connected me with the public school system program for early detection of developmental problems. They evaluated him and told me it looked like he had attention problems. If they offered suggestions, I don't recall them being clear at all. Maybe this was a form of denial? All of this was very upsetting. I felt very lost since I didn't understand how, at the age of three, they could predict that my son's attention span would present a future problem. Fear, which led to worry, became a constant. I remember leaving that evaluation and taking my little boy to the annual Flower Market (fair) and walking around holding his hand thinking, "What if something is wrong? What will I do?" I looked at the other children running and enjoying the rides and thought "Why can't he be settled like they are? Why does there even have to be the hint of a problem?"

That afternoon, I discussed the findings with Rick and Ricky's doctor. The doctor suggested that Ricky was just extremely bright, especially verbal, and that maybe the preschool wasn't a good match…after all, he reminded me, "Ricky can recite the entire Star Spangled Banner perfectly and he is only three." My husband was just as perplexed and without any concrete suggestions.

CHAPTER 1 – STRUGGLE

Rick and I decided to stay with the same preschool. The next fall Ricky would just turn four. Maybe a little maturity, a few new teachers, and adding one more day a week would make a difference. I really connected much better with this year's teachers. However, I again noticed that Ricky's projects looked different from the other children's when they were all drying in the hall at pickup time. The candle project stands out in my memory. The children were shown how to paste construction paper candle strips in a row and draw in the flame at the top to form a pretty candelabra in many colors. Ricky's was the only one whose candles did not form a row and of the few flame tips he was able to scribble, not one was anywhere near the top of the candles. They were all off to the side of the paper. It was a pretty empty feeling to recognize the difference. Come midyear conference time, the feedback confirmed my growing fear. "Further evaluation would be beneficial to Ricky." I was trying to take these reports with a stiff upper lip, but each time, I felt more and more emotional. I always felt so self-conscious when I left because I cried. Now I was really worried.

In the meantime, Rick and I had been trying to have another child. Again, we were having no luck. So we were working through secondary infertility, which actually was more frustrating than the first round because we had been able to conceive once…why not again? I was also a little more affected because it was determined to be my problem, not Rick's. I had also started to do free-lance public relations and advertising work during Ricky's preschool hours to keep up professionally and help with family finances. So there was a good bit of stress involved in my life.

I decided I had to do something more for Ricky so I called the pediatrician again. "Isn't there someone you can recommend who could independently look at our child and give us a third party opinion?" He referred me to a psychologist/learning disabilities specialist who was skilled in administering educational evaluations.

So far, this evaluation was the hardest thing we went through. Not only was it an adult-type office environment but Ricky was evaluated for a little over two hours. That's a long time for a four year old. It was eternity for me. Ricky had to use the bathroom so many times. It concerned me that he was probably using it as a distraction because he couldn't perform the tests. All I could think of was how this gave me just an inkling into

CHAPTER 1 – STRUGGLE

what parents who have very sick children must go through while they are waiting for the diagnosis. You feel very helpless. I prayed for strength for him and for me and told myself it was in God's hands – the way Ricky was made – and I would live with it, deal with it, and help with it in whatever way I could.

Finally the doctor and Ricky emerged for good. The doctor asked me to come into her study to discuss her preliminary findings. Talk about feeling totally overwhelmed and tense! The anxiety over the wait and what she had to say had me tied up in knots. I was trying to keep it together for Ricky's sake. I needed him to know how proud I was of him for completing the testing, and I wanted to seem calm and not overly concerned. All of that came apart when the doctor explained that Ricky did, indeed, have problems. As usual, I began to cry. She told me he had definite attention problems and that medication would probably help. She also said he showed signs of learning problems, that he had difficulty with his motor skills, and that he couldn't seem to get his pencil to do what his mind wanted it to do. She thought he was probably quite bright, however, as he scored in the superior range on the vocabulary tests. She explained that those tests were usually a good indicator of verbal cognitive functioning. She also told me that he exhibited a low level of frustration tolerance (hello?) as he engaged in many work avoidance behaviors. I heard the words and I was heartbroken. I sobbed as I took notes. Again, I felt self-conscious for crying. The doctor assured me I was not the only mother to express my pain through tears, as evidenced by the two boxes of tissues strategically placed next to the chair in which I sat.

I gathered up my four year old and drove home, feeling numb. I just kept thinking, "What becomes of a smart child who can't learn?" "What are we going to do?" As soon as I got Ricky engaged in something so I could have a little privacy, I called and cried to Rick. Then I called the the pediatrician again. "Here's what the specialist said…what does it all mean…should I be giving my four year old son attention medication?" The pediatrician decided he wasn't comfortable just putting Ricky on medication without knowing what was going on or what was causing the problem, so he referred me to a pediatric neurologist.

On to the neurologist. After his evaluation, he told me he thought Ricky was actually quite bright but that he

CHAPTER 1 – STRUGGLE

had some wiring problems in his brain. The way he explained it made some sense. He didn't want to try putting Ricky on attention medication yet. He thought that a couple of years at a special, private school – like The Pilot School – would help Ricky get on track. OUCH! These diagnoses really hurt. During this results session and my ensuing crying jag, I decided it wasn't a very smart idea to keep going to all of these evaluations without Rick. For four years now, I felt it was my responsibility…I only worked part-time so I could care, full-time, for Ricky. Rick had a fairly demanding job and this part was my job. NO MORE! We're talking serious stuff and it was becoming harder for me to hold it together after each appointment. Also, it was more and more difficult to re-explain to Rick what all these experts were telling me. I was not exactly "up" on the functions of the brain as they relate to learning – or as they relate to much at all for that matter!

I was particularly upset with this round because the neurologist had suggested The Pilot School. When I was growing up, the boy next door, whom I had perceived to be mentally handicapped, went to The Pilot School. How could it be that my precious boy was on this level? I was distraught.

As usual, I called the pediatrician. This time I spoke to the nurse practitioner because the doctor was not in – and would not be for several days. As you can figure by now, I needed to talk to somebody because you guessed it – I was crying! She was a gift from heaven. She realized that my biggest concern was that The Pilot School was for mentally handicapped children. She explained that the real focus of the school was on children with normal intelligence who had learning disabilities and needed a lot of special attention to unlock their potential. She told me, coincidentally, that her son had attended the school and was now in college and working toward his pilot's license! She explained that the classes at the school were very small to give the children the amount of individual attention they needed. That calmed me to a point. The next step would be to see if Ricky could be accepted into this very expensive, very small school, known for its long waiting list.

For many reasons, I felt bad. Where did I get this bias toward mentally handicapped children? I am a volunteer for The Delaware Foundation for Enriching the Lives of Persons with Mental Retardation. My mother had taught mentally handicapped children. I certainly knew better! Why had I felt that way? I guess things are different when they hit so close to home. I was going to have to work hard at not letting the "stigma" of having a child with learning problems discolor our world. I rationalized that of course all of this would be difficult to deal with; after all, just look at all of the articles and ads with which we parents are bombarded about how to make our children the best they can be…athletics, music, dance, art lessons, classes and programs for this and that…and that's all extra-curricular. I was faced with a boy who had serious trouble with the basics. He was on a different level and I would have to to get used to it.

I was a runner before Ricky was born and I eventually got back to it. You should have seen me on my runs. Just the mere thought of Ricky's problems or a song playing in my headphones that hit a "chord" and on I'd run, bawling my eyes out. Why him? Why us? How did this happen? What will become of him? That kind of thinking beats you up. It took me a while before I was strong enough to stop it.

Meanwhile, I anxiously tried to get Ricky enrolled in The Pilot School. Lots of phone calls and meetings. They needed to visit his preschool; more evaluations, waiting, worrying, praying, and always crying – although I tried my best to lose it in private, away from Ricky. The two biggest concerns during this two-month process were – would he be accepted (because we had already determined that this was absolutely the single most important thing he needed) and the money. This school would cost more than if we were sending him to the University of Delaware, Rick's and my alma mater -- as if Ricky were living, eating, and attending with a full-time college course load! Almost unbelievable. Rick and I really struggled with this. We did not have that much money just sitting in the bank! We couldn't have planned for this. A child not yet five years old would need more than it would cost for college? But, as we discussed over and over, what good would our college fund do if Ricky wasn't able to learn now? Could we use it to get him started? Sure, but with substantial penalties. Nevertheless, the decision was made. He'd go to The Pilot School no matter what – as long as they could find a spot for him. We would pay for it some way!

At the same time that we were going through all of this with Ricky, we were still toiling through secondary infertility. After several procedures and operations – on

CHAPTER 1 – STRUGGLE

me – oh woe is me…my Ob Gyn concluded that our best chance would be to go with in vitro fertilization. I was referred to that specialist. As pained as we had been all those years trying to conceive Ricky, and with this latest round of infertility – this referral was pretty timely. How in our right minds could we put ourselves through in vitro at a time when Ricky needed so much? It was clear now that I would have to go back to work full time to help afford his school. Even if in vitro was successful, our second child could not receive the time and attention that Ricky had because it was evident now that Ricky had special needs which would require as much attention as we could give. Okay, finally a decision that was obvious. We'd just have to forego in vitro and see what happened. This baby-producing part of our lives was really not going well. I hate to use cliches but, if it was meant to be then it would be. I have strong spiritual beliefs so that made the decision easier. If child number two was to be a reality then it would happen just like Ricky – naturally.

After a two-month wait – which seemed more like two years – the director of The Pilot School informed us that they would have a place for Ricky in the fall. She explained that he would be the youngest child in the youngest class – therefore the youngest child in the school – but they thought he would be okay and this placement was the best thing for him at this point in his development. I thanked the Lord that day. At least we would have him in a place that would help us understand him and help us help him.

My Business Challenge

We decided it would be almost impossible for me to go back to work full time for an employer. The Pilot School had no transportation and no after school care. Ricky would just be turning five. He had so much trouble with transitions and was so often out-of-sorts. How could he lose me on top of all of this? Another obvious solution presented itself. I should work to get my part time, free-lance business built up to the equivalent of full time and make it work so I had the flexibility to transport Ricky and be there for him after school. Thank God I had a profession that I could convert to this type of arrangement and thank God I had the confidence in my skills after working professionally for so many years. It was a GO! While Ricky finished up his last few weeks in preschool, I developed a plan to make it work.

CHAPTER 1 – STRUGGLE

It took the whole family. It took friends and referrals. It took what one old business colleague said when I told him I was starting the business "a lot of guts." I was so very, very fortunate! The clients for whom I had already been doing free-lance work asked me for proposals to do more work. A fellow volunteer from The Delaware Foundation for Enriching the Lives of Persons with Mental Retardation referred me to someone looking for a marketing communications consultant and I eventually got that account. Then, on the very day that Ricky was accepted to The Pilot School, I received a phone call from an old college classmate who is a principal in one of our state's largest and most reputable construction firms. He explained how he had seen the announcement about starting my business in the newspaper and how his company had been discussing the possible need for someone like me. His wife had also told him that I was starting the business. She was an acquaintance of mine from the health club where we both worked out, and we had gotten to know each others' children. He and I talked business and I offered to just come in and talk to his group about what their needs were and how my skills could help. He ended the conversation very compassionately by asking about Ricky. I'm convinced that it wasn't my talent alone that helped me secure this account, which became my most significant. I believe this man was aware of what my family was up against and decided to help! That's the story of how the business got started. It's a story about a lot of people who cared!

Now, don't get me wrong. It wasn't charity. I had to work hard to prove myself and I had to deliver! This "Mommy's running a business" thing changed our family dynamics quite considerably.

First and foremost, I needed help with Ricky so I could work. We had a whole summer in front of us. My parents pitched in and took care of Ricky two days a week throughout the summer at their house, which was several hours away at the beach. To our surprise, Ricky did very well with this. I know it exhausted my parents, but they never complained. They were our biggest support! Also, for one day, every other week, I had a college student, who knew Ricky, take care of him at our home so I could go to meetings.

With the logistics of Ricky squared away, I could concentrate on the actual business itself. Aside from fumbling through the installation of my computer system – I had always had a secretary and was from an era when we were not educated on computers – I did pretty well. It felt good to build something, to help my clients grow. I remember saying over and over again how I didn't know what I'd do without the business, because at least I felt I was accomplishing something. With all the worry, stress and conflict over "what was with Ricky," life had become pretty bleak. I had anxiety over the business, too, but it was more of the type over which I felt I had some control.

Now the flip side of my success with the business was the toll it took on the family and on me. As the business grew, my time was pressed, to say the least. Rick and Ricky were accustomed to sitting down to a home-cooked meal just about every night. I washed, starched and ironed Rick's business shirts. I attended his business functions as a good "corporate wife." I filled the very traditional role of wife and mother. It worked, and I enjoyed it when I wasn't working full-time. It wasn't so easy when I was running the business but I continued to try to do it all. I would work, go to meetings, research Ricky's learning problems, try to squeeze in a workout, pick up Ricky from school, take him to occupational therapy – as this was determined to be a huge need once we got him started at The Pilot

School but something that the school did not offer – try to work in my home office after school with Ricky there needing attention, make dinner, starch the shirts, go to the grocery store…you get the picture. I was always in a rush. All of this with constant conflict between Rick and me over how to parent Ricky – what was wrong with Ricky?

The first thing to go was my work outs. Not a smart choice. As the pace of my life grew faster and faster and my release valves began to close, my stress level grew to hazard status. I was catching colds all the time. I was absolutely exhausted beyond words but had trouble sleeping. I literally did not have a spare second in the day to do anything!! I was getting it all done but compromising my physical and mental health in the meantime. No time for friends, no time to even keep up with business journals let alone read a leisure magazine or cook book. Every now and then when I absolutely could not take it anymore and Rick and I were dangerously at odds, I would call Rick's mother and ask her to take Ricky overnight so Rick and I could get things back into perspective. Rick's mom helped a lot back then. So did my mom and dad. I haven't a clue where we would have been without our family.

CHAPTER 1 – STRUGGLE

Strained Relationships

So Rick and I were at odds. We loved each other – and still do! We had a close relationship. We tried to have fun together, run together, keep current with each other's work issues and help each other…we were supportive of each other. Rick would always say, "it isn't us…it's him!"(Ricky) and I would say "him is us!"

Ricky was so very unique. He was – and is handsome. To look at him and to listen to his vocabulary, he was brilliant! But to live with him and to try to direct his behavior was just about impossible. Rick really couldn't and didn't play with Ricky. Ricky's motor skills were poor. He couldn't catch or throw a ball or ride a bike or do the sporty stuff five or six year old boys did. This disappointed his dad. Rick was an athlete growing up. Ricky "played" on a soccer team when he was five. It wasn't too much fun for him and it was almost unbearable for us. Although few five year olds know what's going on, Ricky was literally lost in space!

Ricky's main pastime was imaginary play. It was elaborate and often excessive. His two favorite roles were a newscaster and a priest. I encouraged it and cultivated it – the costumes, the information to make it authentic. I knew in my heart that this was his strength. As long as it came from his brain and out of his mouth, he was in control. Add a motor component to it and it was lost. So after five years, his creativity was off the charts – and it still is…he really knew his stuff. But to dear old dad, who wasn't able to spend as much time with him and therefore didn't understand him as well, this excessive pretending was especially annoying. And sometimes, if Rick would be honest, it was disappointing because Ricky never played with anyone…he pretended by himself – or occasionally with me – and it was just another reminder of Ricky's differences.

Behavior was even a more difficult situation. Ricky had enormous trouble with transitions. Just stopping to eat or leave the house resulted in major upheavals. He would have tirades over the simplest things – putting on a different shirt or pair of socks or a different snack would set him off, and I mean off! For three straight years the child <u>had</u> <u>to</u> wear a navy blue sweater – every day – summer too! If something set him off, he would howl and flail. We called it flipping out or going into orbit. It was as if electrical sparks were emanating from him – you know that science experiment where you

CHAPTER 1 – STRUGGLE

touch the ball of static electricity and your hair stands up and you feel weird all over? Well, there was no ball and this was no experiment. The electrical sparks were coming from inside his brain! He was in orbit a lot. It really made us feel inadequate as parents because we could not rationally help our son control his behavior.

Ricky could not sleep much past six a.m. no matter what. As I mentioned earlier, it had always been this way. Often he was up even earlier. Once he was awake, he was AWAKE. This was particularly aggravating on Saturday mornings when we did not have to get up for work, school or church. And he was LOUD. It seemed as though his perception of sound was off. If we ran the vacuum cleaner, he would try to yell above it the entire time it was on. Whew…times were tough. We were very often an unhappy, unsettled family.

Tougher still was Rick's and my reaction, as a couple, to all of this. I always needed and wanted to talk about it, to seek help, to make things better. I was often sad. Rick, on the other hand, just wanted the turmoil to go away. He was sick of it. He would often say, "I shouldn't have to live like this – I hate it!" He didn't want to talk about Ricky's problems every day. He often felt that Ricky could control himself but he didn't. I often felt that Ricky couldn't control himself or he would. I grew up in a "make things better, nurturing environment." Rick unfortunately grew up in a tumultuous environment – something I know he was trying to eliminate in our own family – and no wonder! I was pretty relentless in needing to do something. I'm sure it was excessive.

We argued about all of this. We yelled. I cried. Rick withdrew. I was overwhelmed, emotional, and worried. I needed help dealing with Ricky's problems and keeping everything in perspective. When Rick and I would go at it, I couldn't fully concentrate on my business. I would talk to my family and close friends. I was scared that I wouldn't be able to hold it together. Sometimes I felt like I was losing it. Often I worried about Ricky's future…what will become of him?

Rick had no joy. He would even say it. "Parenthood brings me no joy." He would frequently leave for work in the morning yelling, "I'll have a better time at work than I have here!" Whew, that one always found me retreating inside the house, sobbing, hurt, and sometimes, though thank God not very often, angry. Often, I would get down on my knees, sobbing, and pray. I wasn't praying for it to all get better and go away. I prayed for strength. We needed strength.

Accumulated Stress

Even though we had Ricky in a wonderful school and in occupational therapy and even though he was making progress at a slow but steady pace, I really did not understand what was wrong with him. The feedback I was getting the first year at The Pilot School, and in therapy, was that his problem was more substantial than first diagnosed. He really, really struggled to use his hands to write or draw or cut. I was told to imagine what it would be like to wear a mitten on my left hand – I am right-handed – and then use it to write or draw or cut. That's what it was like for Ricky. He had a lot of trouble learning the alphabet, but he eventually did through one-on-one music therapy! I was told in occupational therapy that Ricky would probably eventually need a vocation where his work would be repetitive – maybe a mail room type job. Oh, how could that be? He was so very intelligent with so much potential locked up inside his brain. What was making it so difficult for him to learn, to live a settled life? I knew it was something neurological, but I did not really understand it.

When Ricky was six years old and in his second year at The Pilot School, things hit rock bottom. He could not attend to anything. If he did start a project, he wasn't able to finish it. He would scream at the top of his lungs and repeat random phrases over and over and over. He would cry – more like a howl – and kick and flail his arms and legs. The poor child was absolutely unbearable to live with and completely beaten up – not literally…although sometimes it was so bad I could have beaten him to an absolute pulp, but didn't. Sometimes I would lose control and yell things I didn't mean – I am not a saint! Most of the time I would put cotton balls in my ears or go into a different part of the house until I could get enough composure to deal with him. I thank God for helping me to remain mentally capable. I feel so very bad for those who cannot keep it under control and actually act out their frustration on their children.

At this point, Ricky was walking around hunched over. His speech had regressed. It was both the pattern of his speech and his pitch. The pitch was so annoying that the children in his class were given a symbol to use

CHAPTER 1 – STRUGGLE

to let him know! He had his fingers in his mouth all the time and he was not as comfortable or friendly in the outside world as he used to be. He chewed the buttons off of his shirts as well as the buttons off the television clicker. His physical health deteriorated. Every three to five weeks he would suffer a fever of 102 and had painful episodes of tonsillitis. His croup attacks became more frequent and frightening. The doctor ran tests for strep, mono, Epstein Barr…all came back negative, thank the Lord. He was on and off antibiotics, which always seemed to negatively affect his being.

Home life was intolerable, to put it mildly. Ricky was endlessly agitated, and argumentative over absolutely everything…clothes, food, play. Family dynamics hit an all time low. Yes, even lower than before. The volcano was about to blow! Remember how I said Ricky would go into orbit? He was now living in orbit with those "electrical sparks" surrounding him. Not only in total distress, but also his imaginary play was so excessive that he would stand on the playground at school, alone, and talk to the sky. Now don't get me wrong – he wasn't delusional – he was just so far out there that the only way he could control his inner brain chaos was to escape into his imaginary world. Not good for socialization at school and cause for alarm with his teacher who flat out told us, at one of many special conferences that year, "I don't know who Ricky is, or even if he does." You know how I always cry after one of these sessions? Well, now I was wailing! I love words, but I have no words to describe how I was feeling. My soul was so very close to breaking. My son's spirit was gone!

To make matters worse, during our latest neurologist appointment, which we had demanded because of all these adverse experiences, the doctor became concerned. It wasn't even solely over what I had reported happening since our last visit. On one of the tests, he became suspicious because of a change, for the worse, in the way Ricky's brain was communicating with his body. He was actually afraid of a degenerative condition. He ordered an MRI of Ricky's brain…he said he really wanted to see what was going on. Needless to say, this wasn't at all what we expected! We knew things were out of control, but never, ever did we even dream anything like this could happen! There is no way to convey the fear – no the panic – that I felt.

It may sound hard to believe, but it gets worse. The MRI was scheduled, although we had to wait several weeks before they could take us. In the meantime, we did everything humanly possible to make sure the insurance company had what they needed well in advance. I received assurance that we were in good shape. Rick and I canceled work for the day of the MRI because Ricky was to be sedated, imaged, and would need recovery time before going home. It was to be a long day. Late the afternoon before the MRI, I received a call from the hospital saying they had not received the pre-certification necessary to perform the test. I lost my mind. I called the doctor, the insurance company, the broker who sold my husband's company the insurance policy...I cried, I pleaded, I tried to understand why. The bottom line was – the insurance company was so backed up with pre-certifications that nothing we could do would move our case up on the list and the appointment was canceled.

I was crushed! Between the time the doctor ordered the MRI and this moment, I had so worked myself up into a fearful state, that I wasn't sure I could actually wait even one more day!

Insurance problems were not new to me. That's why I even knew the broker who handled the account! You see, the insurance company had not been covering Ricky's occupational therapy. We had been paying thousands of dollars out-of-pocket. I even suggested they just charge us for the darn MRI! Because of the expense, and the fact that it was covered, the hospital wouldn't even look at that as an option!

I'll break the suspense. Ricky eventually had the MRI. I do not even remember how I made it through the ensuing weeks, except I do remember actually crying, out of nowhere, while I was meeting with a client over a simple newsletter project. I was so embarrassed after the fact, but I had absolutely no control when it happened! It took six weeks from the time the doctor ordered the MRI until we finally got word from Ricky's doctor that the results were negative! Talk about opposing emotions! One minute shaking with pure fear, the very next, screaming with unadulterated joy!

However, the doctor still had concerns over Ricky's backsliding and based on everything that had been going on, he suggested we should try the ever so controversial drug, Ritalin. It really wasn't a hard decision

CHAPTER 1 – STRUGGLE

for us. By this time, we had the recommendation of Ricky's school, his occupational therapist, his psychologist – I'll explain that – and now the neurologist. Okay, it was clearly worth the trial they all suggested.

Before we could get this latest appointment with the neurologist, things had gotten so bad that I researched psychological help for Ricky. First I tried the school, hoping that the school psychologist would see us and offer us some assistance. But the school referred me to several outside psychologists so we could choose one that worked best for us. Another overwhelming experience, because as we were going through the search, I had convinced myself that not only was Ricky suffering from a degenerative brain disorder, but he was also suffering from childhood depression. Yep! I read several articles on the symptoms and worried myself over the fact that depression does run in my Dad's side of the family. That was it. We needed more help!

So, just to re-cap. At this point, we're now dealing with a wonderful, helpful, special school with only six to seven students per teacher, a speech therapist, an occupational therapist, a music therapist, a psychologist, and a neurologist, all trying very hard to get a handle on

ACCUMULATED STRESS

"What's with Ricky." You can't imagine how many times I heard, "What's with Ricky?" Thinking back, the very first time I was ever approached about a possible problem with Ricky, it was his first preschool teacher who actually used those same exact words! I surely wish I knew what, indeed, was "with Ricky."

So many unhealthy emotions swirled through my mind – every day it was something. One day I cried – surprised? – just watching the neighborhood children board the school bus. It saddened me that Ricky couldn't ride a bike and didn't play outside with other children. Even at church I'd sob. Certain hymns would touch me too closely. Rick would look at me, almost embarrassed, and say, "What's wrong now?" A well-meaning fellow parishioner who had known me since I was a child asked if we needed help to have Ricky's back corrected. Remember I told you he was hunching? Well, for some reason it was particularly bad on Sundays. Of all places to feel uncomfortable! Rick and I were so overly conscious now. Ricky actually looked like there was something wrong. Unintentionally we all compared Ricky to others. This only made things worse and added to the fear that had been growing inside me over what will be…

CHAPTER 1 – STRUGGLE

The overwhelming worry over Ricky, the conflict between Rick and me, the press on my time to run my business and perform while dealing with all of the rest of this…the constant rush was hurting my soul and it was finally beginning to break. The connection between the mind, the body, and the soul is absolute.

The final straw came one cold, snowy morning. The family who was to car pool Ricky into school called and said they were not going to drive it that day. Bless their hearts. They lived thirty minutes south of us and we still had about thirty minutes from our house to school. They had driven that distance for their son for the last five years. I didn't blame them for not driving that day. Rick was out of town and I had a very important presentation to make to a client. Ricky's school was open in spite of the snow so I would have to drive him. I made a big mistake. The interstate was backed up so badly that I would never get him to school and get to my meeting in time if I didn't try another way. I went by the back roads and shouldn't have – my car was not good in the snow. I crested a hill going only about twenty-five m.p.h. but wind had iced the road and I lost control of the car. We slid into a ditch and hit a fence. It was like slow motion. There was nothing I could do except tell Ricky we would be okay, we were going too slowly to get seriously hurt. We were both terribly frightened when we landed. We were not hurt, but the car was. I would need a tow truck to pull it out. In the meantime, poor Ricky was really upset about it and worried about getting to school. No sooner did I get him safely out of the car there appeared a kind and generous man offering to help. My first thought was to get Ricky to school so he would not be distressed by the tow truck and commotion. The man drove us to school while I used his cell phone to call my client and explain that I'd be late or not be there at all. Then the man drove me back to the accident scene.

My Revelation

It didn't happen on the spot. It was cold, I was alone, there were so many things I had to do. Once the immediate situation passed, it became clear to me. It was as if the car accident was a manifestation of all that had been going on in my life…"You are on a collision course. You've got to slow down!" I heard the message!

Understanding

As I plodded along after the accident, knowing I needed to slow down…to simplify…I read a few self-help books that really affirmed the need. There were so many good suggestions on how to live more fully – I remember thinking, "I must really be in bad shape, I don't remember the last time I read a women's magazine or tried a new recipe or went out with my girlfriends." I put slow down at the top of my list of internal commands – but my wanting to and being able to were not in sync.

It took time, but I did get myself balanced. Once you live through something and have the advantage of looking back, you learn. And what I learned was the unbelievable power of understanding. That, alone, made the difference. I hope it will be the most important thing you remember from reading this book. Everything else comes together once you understand.

But when we were living through our most difficult period, I didn't know that if I just understood Ricky's neurological problem to the best of my ability, everything else would fall into place. It just evolved. But now I do know it – absolutely – and I share it with you so that your period of struggle might be shortened. That's one of the advantages of somebody else going first. It's

CHAPTER 2 – UNDERSTANDING

one of the gifts I give to you from my struggle. You must understand the struggle before you can help it.

So there we were struggling along. Ricky was totally overwhelmed and so many wonderful specialists were trying to help. The dear child was getting extra one-on-one adaptive physical education at school, I had the occupational therapist actually going into his school, I was taking Ricky out of school early for psychologist appointments, we were trialing Ritalin, you name it…we were doing it. All the while, we were walking wounded. Rick, Ricky and myself. We were getting up and going through the motions of life each day but we were beaten up.

Each week, for a year and a half, I had been taking Ricky to an hourly occupational therapy (O.T.) session off-site after school. I had learned that this was very important for him. Just so you understand, O.T. was designed to help people with neurological handicaps form adaptive responses that enable them to improve their own condition. Ricky's therapist would creatively work to organize his central nervous system through activities that seemed like play to him. Every week I would sit behind a two-way mirror in a closet that contained a chair and a speaker. I could see and hear into his therapy room, but he could not see me. He would lie in a harness attached to the ceiling and swing. He would move his body through obstacle courses, and play with tools meant to improve his fine motor coordination and strength. I watched, I cried, I was amazed at how hard simple things were for him. For example, it was not possible for him to stack two blocks side by side and lay one on top to form a simple tower even with the therapist patiently showing him how to do it with her own set of blocks! He was five years old! He could tell you who the President of the United States was but he couldn't build a tower with three blocks! He cognitively understood so much for his age but was able to perform so little. I knew his motor skills were a big problem, but I did not understand why.

Finally, after a year and a half of weekly therapy sessions, his skill level was to a point where his therapist could perform a very lengthy evaluation called the SIPT Test. It didn't mean much to me until I was able to observe Ricky during the testing in a special tiny room while following along in a manual his therapist had written for parents. I did not know it at the time but this testing session was the beginning of my understanding.

The manual described what each sub-test was and explained why the ability to perform the individual task

CHAPTER 2 – UNDERSTANDING

was important and, in certain instances, the ramifications if the child did not have ability in that area.

Well, I ate it up! This was the first thing I could start to wrap my brain around. I asked what SIPT meant. "Sensory Integration and Praxis," of course! What is that? All the therapy words were foreign to me. My eyes were opened. I started to understand how substantial Ricky's problems were. It blew my mind to see just how much trouble he had. No wonder he was always flipping out! I would too if I understood so much, but could do so little!

Once I was back in the regular observation closet, I saw an article from a periodical called "Sensory Integration Quarterly" hanging on the wall. I asked the therapist if there was a book or anything I could get my hands on about this topic because I had seen for myself during the evaluation that Ricky definitely struggled in all areas tested. She told me about A. Jean Ayres, the pioneer in the area of Sensory Integration, and a book she wrote almost twenty years ago. I researched it, I found it, I waited patiently for it to come in.

The day the bookstore called, I dropped everything to go get the book. I was so excited. I can remember trying to drive to pick up Ricky at school and read it at every stop light. Talk about the proverbial lights coming on – we're talking flood lights – the bulbs were on and the information was directed right at us! Connections between what was written and Ricky's behavior were ASTOUNDING!

I so remember reading the preface of that book that every time I even think of it I get goose bumps. I have to include it. It makes the point about understanding. This preface, and some of the following explanations of Sensory Integration are from *Sensory Integration and the Child* by A. Jean Ayres, Ph.D.:

> Mothers of children with problems carry a tremendous emotional load. Few occupations carry as much, and those that do, carry a different kind. Fathers of neurologically handicapped children do not escape from the burden, but they carry it differently.
>
> Sometimes the weight of the problem seems too much to bear, and the presence or severity of the problem is denied in order to cope. Or parents recognize the severity and they search and search for better answers to a difficult situation.
>
> This book will not end that search, for it does not have all the answers; but it will give many parents the opportunity to understand their child better. The greater the understanding of a problem, the more effectively it is helped. This book was written to promote that understanding.

CHAPTER 2 – UNDERSTANDING

"The greater the understanding of a problem, the more effectively it is helped." Sounds pretty simple, but in reality, at least for us, it took us over three years to truly understand our son and it made all the difference in the world!

The most important thing I learned right away was that I was not a bad mother. Seriously! You might say, "How in the world could you think you were a bad mother with all you and your husband were doing for that child?" Well, when you don't understand why your child is acting the way he does and why he has such unbelievable trouble learning, it is easy to conclude that you must not be doing it right! I can't tell you the relief I felt after paging, only briefly, through that book. Incidents since birth came pouring back to me and now seemed to have reason – boy, we could use some reason! We understood that Ricky had a problem and we knew we were doing all we could. What we did not understand was the problem itself – monumental difference!

Well, the problem itself was complicated. Complicated to understand, complicated to explain, and certainly complicated enough for us to realize, pretty quickly, that it wasn't something that was going to be fixed – maybe improved – but Ricky would probably live with it for the rest of his life.

Ricky's sensory integration system was not working normally. Actually it was quite dysfunctional. Sensory integration is the brain's ability to interpret and organize information from the senses – vision, hearing, taste, smell, touch, balance, gravity, body position and movement. Sensory integration occurs naturally in most people, so we tend to take it for granted – just as we take our heartbeat or digestion for granted. Well, when the brain is not processing sensory input properly, it usually is also not directing behavior effectively. Think of the brain as a large city and of neural impulses as the automobile traffic in the city. Good sensory processing enables all the impulses to flow easily and reach their destination quickly. Sensory integration dysfunction is like a "traffic jam" in the brain. We've all been in traffic jams, so I know you can at least imagine what this might be like.

So that is elementary sensory integration. Thanks to Jean Ayres for explaining it so simply. But within this world we found certain areas that were more troublesome than others. Praxis – remember that weird word I threw out during his SIPT testing? It's a biggie. It is another major thing we take for granted because it's programmed into the normal brain; it is automatic. Well, there was faulty programming when it came to Ricky's brain. What is it? Praxis is motor planning, which is the ability of the brain to conceive of, organize and carry out a sequence of unfamiliar actions.* I'll give you an example. Ricky would get seriously overwhelmed when asked to clean up his toys. Even though he could see the crates where his toys belonged, it was impossible for him to "plan" what he should do to get the toys into the crate. Another example – his therapist would ask Ricky to get from point A to point B without touching the floor. He was supposed to use the therapy equipment to swing, climb, or roll the distance. He could not figure out a way, without her verbal instructions and physical help, to move his body through this "no floor challenge."

Motor planning is the first step in learning new skills. Good motor planning requires accurate information from all of the sensory systems of the body.* A problem with this most basic function would be reason enough for Ricky to have trouble learning!

We also found out that his body awareness system was faulty. That's when sensations from your joints and muscles give your brain information on what your body is doing. It is extremely important to fine and gross motor activities.* Additionally, his inner sense of balance wasn't "up to snuff" either.

Ricky's visual-spatial perception was also "out-of-order." Visual-spatial perception is how a person perceives the relationship of external space to his body as well as how he perceives objects in space relative to other objects.* Children automatically program their brains, through play, by moving under, over, around and through objects. These perceptual foundations are the basis for their ability to mentally label space – you know – left, right, above, and below.*

That was just the occupational therapy analysis. Thanks to Sensory Integration International's <u>Understanding Sensory And Motor Challenges In The Classroom</u> booklet for the above* definitions.

The neurologist's assessment added congenital Gerstmann Syndrome – now called Right Brain Dysfunction – which includes substantial abnormalities in writing, calculating, differentiating left from right, localizing ones fingers in space, and problems with constructional tasks.

CHAPTER 2 – UNDERSTANDING

No wonder Ricky was always in orbit, falling out of his chair, couldn't ride his bike, had trouble throwing balls and writing, coloring, cutting, knowing left from right or up from down. No wonder learning was so unbelievably difficult. No wonder he was frustrated, maybe even depressed, argumentative, impossible.

No wonder he wailed when I rocked him as a baby. His inner sense of balance and gravity were off. Something that soothed most babies probably horrified his system. No wonder stroller rides ended the way they did, and he got stuck in the McDonald's Playland wailing when everybody else was having a great time. No wonder he would scream bloody murder during a hair cut and gag at certain foods' texture or smell. No wonder he screamed over the sound of the vacuum cleaner. No wonder he wore the same damn navy blue sweater for three straight years…good grief, no wonder he was sooooo unsettled. I'd escape to some imaginary world and talk to the sky, too, if this was the chaos I lived in!

You can't begin to know how much I have learned from all of this. I am not just talking about the specifics of his disability. I'm talking about what I have learned about <u>all</u> <u>of</u> <u>us</u> – not one of us has a pure system. Some of us are organized and some of us are not. I am. I used to get very frustrated with business associates who are not. Now I have tolerance. Now I know what a remarkable gift I was given.

I ask my friends to celebrate their children who are normal learners or who have natural athletic ability. I try to let them know just how much goes into learning and the good motor coordination necessary for athletics, just how complex all of it really is. Please don't take it for granted. It is a gift. You need to know it! Not just your child's ability, but also your own!

Needless to say, once I had digested all of this information, I wanted to educate everybody – especially Ricky! We were very honest with him all along. We told him that he had a neurological difference that made it difficult for him to learn like most kids but that was about all we could tell him. My mantra was, "We're all different and everybody has something. It's okay." Now I could try to explain.

I wanted my family to understand. Everyone gave us support, but nobody really understood what was going on or why. As I mentioned, my mother had

CHAPTER 2 – UNDERSTANDING

taught mentally handicapped children, so she had endless patience with Ricky. She was perplexed, concerned, but patient. Rick's mom, bless her heart, was your black and white type and Ricky was so far in the gray area that she would just get downright mad at him. Because he was so smart, she figured…there was nothing wrong with him, he just needed a good swift kick in the butt. Dear Gran was of the stern Irish-Catholic persuasion – bless all of you – and she just wasn't going to have any of this! In spite of being so frustrated with Ricky, she loved him and would spend a lot of time with him. She knew Rick and I needed the break. The two of them were a pair! Gran died a few years ago and we miss her. We talk about those times and the things she would say and do out of not understanding and they seem funny now. They were not funny back then. Gran was very important to Ricky and he very much wanted to please her. It was a tough task. But everything was pretty tough back then.

Being a communicator by profession, I wrote a paper about Ricky's neurological system for my family, the school, the psychologist, friends…for anyone I thought should understand Ricky. I wrote it for his father. I tried to impart all I had seen and now understood so that home life might improve. I prayed that we might be able to adjust our expectations surrounding Ricky's behavior – and our reactions to him – now that we understood, and from that would come more patience. We desperately needed more patience.

The Mind, Body & Soul Connection

Another thing I learned, after looking back, was the absolute connection between the mind, body and soul. This was a live-through/learn-from revelation and one that comes second only to the understanding of Ricky's actual neurological problems in terms of what was necessary to put our family on the path to wholeness.

You've read about the many factors stressing our family. For over six years we had been living in a constant state of strain. There was so much worry, conflict, and fear over what was and what would be. I didn't see it at the time but all of this stress was making us sick – literally and figuratively – and was only adding to the difficulty of our lives.

I know there has been so much written about stress and the immune system. I'll simplify all the research – if

CHAPTER 2 – UNDERSTANDING

you are stressed, especially over a prolonged period, your immune system becomes suppressed and you get sick more often.

All of this is so crystal clear now that I look back but it was not at all obvious when we were living through it. I had never been so sick in my life until Ricky was born. I don't mean seriously ill, I mean persistently not well – mostly headaches, colds, increased seasonal allergies, then sinus infections and bronchial issues…you get the idea.

And how about Ricky? He was constantly sick as a baby. I'm sure the fact that his brain was not able to process sensory input efficiently put an enormous stress on his system and it took its toll physically. And then remember when he fell apart and was sick and hunched over all the time? He was so unbelievably frustrated by understanding everything yet not being able to perform, that he emotionally and physically went down. This time it was his more sophisticated soul that was as much to blame as his brain!

Same went for me! At first my health issues stemmed from the simple stresses of motherhood – lack of sleep, lack of a job description. Things got worse as my life grew more complex and my broken soul was added to the equation. The deeper and longer the worry, the more persistent the little health issues became. I knew I was taking way too much Tylenol, and I didn't want to!

I cannot explain why Rick did not seem to suffer with as many health problems as Ricky and I did. For one, we're talking about a man who has never missed a day of work due to illness and for another, I don't think he carried the deep worry as far as I did. Please know, he was extremely concerned. I just don't think most men/fathers "carry it the same way," as Jean Ayres stated. I'm thankful he was physically healthy and I'm thankful that he didn't carry the worry as far as I did. It was obviously unhealthy!

Now, what to do about all of this?

Action

WHAT TO DO ABOUT RICKY?

Remember how I told you that truly understanding Ricky's problem was what made <u>the</u> difference? That it was an evolution, and when I looked back I could see it? Well the same thing happened with what to do about Ricky. It wasn't as if while we were living through it, the answers were apparent, it was a natural progression based on clearly understanding his problem.

And guess who gave us the first clue on what to do? It was six-year old Ricky himself. At the time, he was being taken out of his classroom for special, adaptive, one-on-one physical education and also for speech therapy. Additionally, I had his occupational therapist coming in once a week to monitor his classroom situation to see where some simple adjustments to his environment would help improve his performance. For instance, his desk chair was too tall for his feet to rest properly on the ground so his feet weren't giving good information to his brain, so a shorter chair was brought in…things like that. AND, once a week, I had to pick him up early for his appointment with the psychologist. We were really trying to do everything we could to help him.

Well, one day during all of this Ricky just let it rip…"this is toooooo much, it's all just toooooo much!"

CHAPTER 3 – ACTION

He made this announcement at school during a special reading group time that was led by the Chairman of the Lower Wing. During our next meeting, she told us about Ricky's declaration. If I hadn't truly understood the state of his neurological system I'm sure I, and the school, would have just kept loading on the special services…but…I did understand what was going on in that brain of his. It was overloaded! It was naturally overloaded to begin with and then we were further overloading it with tooooo much help!

So I asked him about it. How was all of this making him feel? Bless his heart, it was making him feel awful. First of all, he said as much as he liked his occupational therapist, he felt dumb having her at school and the "stupid baby chair" made him feel like a baby. Everybody else had regular chairs and his was stupid. He was overwhelmed by being taken out of regular classes so often and it was all just tooooo much, just like he said!

We adjusted his special services. Understanding that his brain was already in a constant traffic jam made it easy to peel away a few of the extras we had heaped on him. Honestly, if I didn't understand, I know I would have absolutely wanted to continue with everything we were doing. My philosophy back then was, the more help we can give him, the more he will progress. Oh, if we could only fix him. I was wrong!

This whole experience was the beginning of my personal understanding of the concept of F-L-O-W. We took action before we understood and we had to make adjustments, actually slow down the amount of help, not increase it. This was going with his flow.

This enlightened me to going with the natural flow of life. I have found that you have to be aware of it, open to it and looking for it in order to go with it. If that sounds a little "out there" to you right now, that's okay! Just don't get turned off by it sounding too philosophical. It's an important piece to the end goal of living wholly.

Now that we really understood Ricky, we made adjustments to a lot of other things, too. Most importantly, we adjusted our expectations. We didn't say to ourselves, "this is so messed up we'll be lucky if he can do X or Y." It wasn't like we lowered our expectations. We adjusted them to fit Ricky. If we would be making a transition from one activity to another, we knew that it would not be easy for him and we were prepared to see him temporarily visit "orbit." The only difference now

CHAPTER 3 – ACTION

was that at least we understood why he flipped out in the first place. You see before, not only would he lose it, but then we would lose it too because it was so unbelievably frustrating! I mean come on – all I would do was call him for dinner – was it really worth a screaming fit? Well, yes, in his jammed up brain, it was his only way.

With the adjustment of our expectations came the need to find a new level of patience. Because now that we understood him, we really had no right to lose it. We had to stay grounded and patiently prepared. We learned the need for and the value of soft, frequent cues that something was going to change. It made a difference. We're talking enormous amounts of patience – I never knew I had – but it helped. You can imagine that our previous rounds of freaking out after he flipped out only made matters much, much worse. It wasn't obvious until we changed our approach, and the difference in his behavior was truly the gift for which I had been praying. When he would lose it, I would bring him close for a tight hug and say, "I understand that this is tough for you. I'm here to help you adjust. Everything is going to be okay." An enormous difference from "All I want you to do is come to dinner. Stop screaming and throwing a fit. You are driving us crazy!" I switched from being against him to understanding him and being on his side. Don't get me wrong, it didn't stop him from losing it because he couldn't just stop, but it certainly helped the outcome considerably.

You might be thinking, well, how much of this behavior was the result of his neurological disability and how much was just him being a child? I cannot begin to tell you how many times we have asked ourselves that same question. The line between the two is very blurry. I can tell you that it became quite clear to me that the majority of Ricky's behavioral troubles stemmed from his frustration with being so smart and knowing what he wanted to do and how he wanted to behave, and his inability to do it. I determined that it was no longer beneficial to continue to see the psychologist when I found myself educating the psychologist about Ricky's neurological disorder and how it impacted his behavior. The answer to his behavioral problems was in helping his neurological system. The key to that was love, understanding, patience, prayer, and continuing at The Pilot School and with his occupational therapy. The psychologist was one more layer of extra service we could let go.

CHAPTER 3 – ACTION

Also, over time it became evident that taking Ricky certain places overstimulated him and caused a lot of unnecessary trouble for all of us. I stopped trying to take him clothes shopping and instead bought things for him and returned them if they didn't fit or were not "just so." As you can imagine, Ricky was pretty particular about clothes – easy on and off because snaps and zippers were too difficult to maneuver, etc. Trips with him to the grocery store were always tough. The lights, sounds, and shelves full of products made him crazy and he would talk very loudly into space the whole trip. I would only take him when I absolutely had to. Also, a regular routine and schedule every day made it much easier for him to manage his behavior and make progress. I made it a point to bring him home directly from school every day so he could get right to his homework. I only ran errands with him after school if it was urgent. He did not participate in any evening activities. He would do his homework, have dinner, play on his computer, have family time and go to bed. We reserved karate and special outings for weekends. Sounds pretty isolating but it worked. It gave him the opportunity to master his world without too much outside distraction. Having his environment as organized as humanly possible helped, too. My gift of strong organizational ability was my life preserver!

Another critical step we took that significantly helped was trying medication. I already mentioned that everyone associated with helping Ricky suggested we at least try Ritalin. Before this we had thought that if we helped his neurological system through therapy and the proper school environment it would help his attention issues. But, as we peeled away the layers of his neurological trouble, it became clear that he had additional, substantial attention problems that would probably benefit from medication. Everyone told me that if the medicine helps, you will see it immediately – like night and day. We tried it during his most difficult period, at age six, and it worked! Most clearly it helped him at school. It improved his ability to attend to everything and we also found it improved his ability to actually write. His small motor ability was greatly enhanced while he was on the medication! His behavior at home was much improved. It was positively clear when he was "on" and when his medication had worn off. It is still that way.

I tell people that when it comes to Ritalin, we were one of the lucky families. First, because Ricky was so

CHAPTER 3 – ACTION

troubled there was no doubt that it was worth a try – he wasn't just a fidgety boy who was borderline. Second, we were lucky because it helped him progress. Aside from adjustments in the amount and some minor side effects like tics and lack of appetite and inability to get to sleep at night, we have had a very good experience with Ritalin. I know it is controversial. Many parents have asked me about our experience. I tell them that I look at it this way – if Ricky could not see very well and needed glasses, we would give him glasses. If Ricky's heart was defective and there was medication that would improve his condition, we would try it. Why, then, wouldn't we try a medication that would help him to learn and to behave? Yes, we worry about the long term effects that are not known. But we would rather give this precious child the quality of life he so profoundly deserves now than worry about what it might some day do to him. Obviously his brain chemistry was missing this necessary stimulant. I thank God there is something that can help him now.

Living now. Going with the flow. Patience. These are lessons I have learned from my struggle with Ricky. It isn't that I have no concern or worry about the future or that I wouldn't like the flow of Ricky's life to somehow be different. It is about dealing with the here and now, being patient, and making the best of today. Because I've also learned that it isn't necessarily true that with enough knowledge or love or prayer or energy anything can be solved. Although I am very knowledgeable about Ricky's problems and I try very hard to help him, I cannot fix his condition. That's control and it is out of my control. The only thing I can control is my reaction to all of this. That's not to say that we will not continue to take action – we will, and it will help.

What To Do About Me?

I can only impart these "words of wisdom" about going with the flow, dealing with the here and now, and being patient because I have learned how. I had to, it was a matter of survival. Hand-in-hand with what we did for Ricky from an action standpoint was what I did for me in terms of trying to balance things out and reduce the level of stress that had accumulated and begun to wreak havoc with my mind, body and soul.

I consciously worked at getting a grip on my worry about what will become of Ricky. The foundation for that was that I understood him better now. I consciously worked at adjusting my client load. I became more

CHAPTER 3 – ACTION

selective and learned that I could say no. The load had become too much and I needed to cut back. I found the confidence to say to myself, "You don't have to take every account that comes your way. Having more balance and the ability to help Ricky become better adjusted is worth more than any money I could receive from more work. As long as we have his tuition and can make ends meet…" I lived through these changes and adaptations by going with the flow – by slowing down and hearing my inner voice through the chaos. Loud and clear the sound from my soul said, "Be easier on yourself. Accept the way things are. Take care of yourself."

Take care of yourself. Self. It starts with you. There is not another person on earth who can – or should – take care of you like you. I believe there is a spirit who will try to get in there and help if you're open – but here on earth, it's up to you!

Your sense of self and how important you are is at the core of everything. I don't mean the egotistical, self-centered kind of self. I mean the very essence of you…all the good stuff. You truly need to find it and believe in it before you can nurture it and grow into wholeness. I figured that out along the way. I'm still finding my good stuff and it feels great! Like anything really good, keeping self as the priority takes hard work and discipline because the demands of life and the many roles we play can get pretty heavy and begin to smother it. But it – self – is absolutely the key.

I'm going to share what I found to be the most important elements involved in taking care of myself and improving my well being. I'm not talking about just keeping myself generally healthy, as in free from colds and sinus infections. I'm talking about healthy in the total sense…not just my body but also my mind and my soul – being alive and feeling really good – at least most of the time. I'm talking about finding real joy in living.

I am fortunate that my interest in health and fitness has been both an avocation – since I was a very young girl – and a professional endeavor. I was already practicing many of the things I'll be preaching. But there were several areas where I needed a good bit more education and a lot more practice!

I'm not going to just list what I think you should do to be healthy and whole. We're all different. Like a recipe, I'll give you the ingredients and how I used them and how they made a difference for me. You might mix the

CHAPTER 3 – ACTION

ingredients in a different order or in different amounts. My goal is to help you learn what I have learned about the connectedness of the mind, body and soul.

Spirit to the Rescue!

First and foremost for me is spirituality. It is central. The sense that there is some force more powerful than me gives me the ability to "lift it up" and seek direction. It's not for another human being to do. It's up to me and the spirit. I am proud of the fact that for me spirituality is organized religion. I am a Christian. That's how I was raised. That's what I know. That's what I believe. That's what I practice. That's what gives me strength and hope. That's why I have persevered.

When you have to rely on you, only you, it can be overwhelming. If you are ultimately in charge, where do you go for that boost of inner nourishment that we all need? Where do you go for the "Big Picture?" I believe that there is a plan. I believe that all that I am and all that I have comes from God. It's a gift and I need to do something good with it! I believe that God is present in my life every day. It's really awesome when you can see it. I can see it because I have been taught to see it and I look for it. I see love, gratefulness, direction, forgiveness, truth, faith, kindness, peace, strength, self-control, generosity, joy, hope, cheerfulness, diligence, wisdom, compassion, friendship, charity, community, comfort, hard work, healing, boldness…and it gives me so much good energy! It is the bright, shining light showing me the way. It is the <u>you</u> <u>can</u> in my life!

If I did not have this faith, I would not have been able to endure my struggles with Ricky and Rick and with running the business. I was taught that suffering is a part of life but that there is always and forever hope. I trust God to show me the way. I believe that God is with me and will help me through this struggle and through all those still to come. I believe that there is a reason for all of this, and I am meant to learn from it, grow from it and share it. That's why I've written this book.

I teach Sunday School. I believe it was important to me growing up and to the person I have become and it is important for Ricky and for children, period. I have found that you really need to be taught to be good, to be caring of others, to be kind, to love, to be forgiving, to be thankful. It is the foundation for integrity and character. It helps to have good role models – parents, family, teachers, and friends. But I have found that you also need a spiritual education and it should start at a young age to make the biggest difference. Like learning, practicing and perfecting a sport. The younger you start, most often, the better you become.

I have learned from my time teaching Sunday School children and then on the other end of the spectrum, from my years in business, that if spirituality and concern for others is not shown and grown, if it isn't taught and nurtured from a young age, then it is not the first thing to which the egotistical self turns.

However, I honestly do believe that it is never too late to start to find or practice your spirituality! It has made and will continue to make the most important difference in my life.

Mental Fitness

Okay, here's one of the areas where I needed help. You've already read about how stressful my life had become, how my physical health had deteriorated and how it was clearly connected to how I was thinking and feeling and how fast I was moving. I knew I needed to simplify, slow down, chill out, stop worrying so much, find balance, get some joy back into my life. I literally had to research ways to do this and then make time to implement and practice them until I found what worked. No small task since I had become used to either limiting or ignoring what I needed. At first I felt guilty about taking time for myself, but once I learned the power and refreshment to be found and the resulting positive effects on my ability to not only help myself but also my family, I was sold.

First and foremost was exercise. I am lucky that this is something I already did and about which I had personal knowledge concerning the positive benefits. Exercise is another ingredient that I will get into in another section shortly but here I just want to say that exercise is essential to mental fitness. All I had to do was reposition exercise back into a place of priority since it had slipped off the top of the list. I had been exercising through all of this, just not as regularly as I needed to reap all of the benefits.

Next, I read and learned about mindfulness and living in the present moment. I had a great time researching eastern religions and cultures. I gained so much from their principles. Simply put, I trained myself to give tasks my undivided attention and to see something positive in even

CHAPTER 3 – ACTION

the most mundane and annoying aspects of life. For instance – and this example takes this point to extremes – I call it my "It's all in how you fold the toilet paper" example. I personally do not enjoy scrubbing the bathrooms in my home each week. Practicing mindfulness, I learned to look at it as a task that I was lucky to be able to perform. I had the strength and tools to do it. It certainly improved both the appearance and cleanliness of our home from a sanitation standpoint. Finally, if we were having company, I sometimes would go so far as to fold the toilet paper into a point when I was done, to show pride in my accomplishment – you know, like they do at nice hotels? Anyway, I take the barbs in stride when asked about what in the world I was thinking when I folded the toilet paper and I use it as an opportunity to make a point – literally – that it's all in the way you look at what you do.

That might be an extreme example, but practicing mindfulness has become a very routine thing for me and it is very helpful. Anytime I feel like I've got to rush through an activity or chore, I think about slowing down and finding something meaningful in what I am doing. Then I try to do it with total focus. I try not to think about what I need to do next and not about what I've already done – just about what I'm doing at the present time.

In addition to mindfulness, I added the powerful element of thankfulness. That simple addition transforms everything! You can always find something for which to be grateful in everything you do. It's not hard and together with mindfulness it is very grounding.

Once I started to slow down and really pay attention to what I was doing, I trained myself to take in whatever I could with as many senses as possible. I concentrated on how things smelled and looked, sounded and felt and of course, tasted. I actually slowed down and tasted my food for the first time in a long time. You sure do miss a lot when you rush and don't pay attention. Simple, ordinary, every day things became much more enjoyable. Lying next to Ricky at night saying prayers, I would consciously smell his damp hair after his shower. I hadn't done that since he was a baby. When Rick would pat me or hold my hand, I would hone in on how wonderful it felt and not take it for granted. Small changes that made a very big difference.

Once I started becoming aware of these things, I noticed just how tense I was. I carried a lot of stress in my shoulder area. I was tight, I could feel it. I worked at

CHAPTER 3 – ACTION

taking deep breaths and releasing the tension. Some days it felt like my shoulders were up to my ears! A few deep breaths and a concentrated effort to drop my shoulders and relax made me feel like a new person. Deep breathing calms the nervous system – it's good for you!

When Rick asked me what I wanted for Christmas I told him all I really wanted was more time to practice all of these new good things and a massage every once in a while. He really wanted to help, so he asked me to find a massage therapist and he would take care of the rest. Bless his heart, he bought me a package of six, one-hour, in-home sessions and I'm not sure I can find the adjective to describe those sessions. Research shows that human touch through massage is healing. Healing – that's the word. In more ways than one! It incorporates touch, smell – aromatherapy oils, and sound – soothing instrumental music. It's really a good time to practice mindfulness. I have taught myself to stay focused only on the body part being worked, the smell and the sound. I tell myself "stop" if I dare let Ricky, the business, or other worries enter this special time.

Another technique you hear a lot about is meditation. I haven't been formally trained to meditate, but for me I use my morning prayer time as a form of meditation to stabilize and start off fresh and hopeful. There is so much power in prayer, I know that it works! I know I could do more in the area of actual meditation and I plan to try. There is only so much time a stressed-out woman can find to de-stress!

Time is another issue. It takes time to work on all of these good things and finding the time takes organization and priority setting. Self-improvement comes at a price – but there is really nothing to lose!

Silence has become very important to me, as has nature. I feel very calmed by quiet, so I seek it out. With all the noise and commotion generated by Ricky's being, and life in general, silence is a sharp and welcome change. Nature – there is so much to gain by paying attention to nature. Seasonal changes…I don't know how many busy, working years flew by and I didn't even take the time to notice, I mean really notice – go outside and "get into it" notice – how beautiful the seasons are. And I spent a lot of time outside running. My favorite form of exercise and I didn't even use the time to notice the colors of fall, the quietness of snow, the glory of spring bursting forth with its new and wonderful sights and the green, green trees and the blue, blue sky and water of summer. Wow – how soothing it can all be. How long has it been since you smelled the thick fragrance of honeysuckle on a warm, dewy morning? It took me all the way back to my childhood! We race around and so often take it all for granted so it's incredibly therapeutic to just stop and take it in. Talk about the big picture. It's really big when you take a minute to look up at the night sky and try to count the stars, or ride a big wave at the beach and get pounded in the sand, or stand on top of a mountain and feel its strength. Again, very simple things. All it takes is a few moments to be mindful and really notice. It changes the rhythm of your life.

What about music? It is said to soothe the soul, right? Well, it does mine! I listen to mellow, jazzy sounds when I need to slow down and fast, bumpy beats when I need to rev up. Music can change my mood and I let it. Same thing with a smile. I learned that just the sheer act of turning up the corners of your mouth can elicit a happy emotional response. So when things are really low and I really need a quick help, I force myself to smile. I might look like a lunatic driving down the interstate by myself with a big smile affixed to my face but hey, it works!

And speaking of lows, we all have them. They are

necessary. It's not realistic to go through life perpetually high on all of life's good things. Life builds in down time – it's to be used for reflection and rejuvenation. You just don't want to get stuck reflecting and not rejuvenate. I know folks who are stuck there and my heart literally aches for them. I can't imagine the pain and suffering.

For me, I had to acknowledge my struggles with Ricky and Rick and the pace of my life. I had to talk about our situation – if you know me you know that I need to talk about it! I had to feel the negative thoughts, the fear and pain so I could then do something about it. And there is nothing like a positive attitude. I really tried to focus on the slow but steady progress and not the numerous issues we still faced. Once I stopped thinking with fear about what might become of Ricky and focused instead on his progress, which with it brought new potential, the load lightened.

Relationships

I just mentioned that I needed to talk about my struggles and joked that for anyone who knows me they know I mean TALK. But where would I be if I couldn't talk to someone? I would be in pretty bad shape and it makes me feel good to know that research indicates that I am not alone. It is widely reported that women, in particular, need to talk things out.

Connecting with others is critical to mental and physical health. Studies abound on the negative consequences of social isolation. We were made to be in relationships!

For me, the most important relationship of all is family. It is the foundation of my life. Without my family and my faith, I would have fallen apart. Even though my relationship with Rick has been strained over Ricky, we are very committed to each other and to doing all we can to keep our family together and healthy. We have each other. We talk and we worry and we work together. We try hard to find time to have fun together. We love each other and we love Ricky very much.

My relationship with my parents is the basis for everything I am. It has sustained me through it all and they continue to nourish me with encouragement. They are always there to help with Ricky. What an absolute blessing. I am so fortunate to still have both of my parents. Relationships with sisters and brothers, even across the miles, are loving and supportive and central to me and to Rick and to Ricky.

Next comes friends! Friends truly rescued me during some of my hardest times. I call a few of my closest girlfriends my angels for their help in opening me back up. Not that I was a total mess, I just wasn't really allowing any time for fun. All I did was work and take care of Ricky and Rick and worry. Again, not paying much attention to me. Well, my angels took care of that. Rick encouraged it. He knew I needed the break. Things had become too serious and he wasn't used to seeing me have no fun. I used to be a fun girl and I was missing. Well, these girls know how to have fun. Once I made the time to be with them and go cavorting and dancing and whooping it up, the seriousness of life seemed to take on a different face. I found out how important it is to put some time into having fun, to balancing the scale a little better – and the results were irresistible! Now when they call and it might not be the easiest outing to arrange, I go the extra mile because in the end it always turns out to be just the right medicine. Who can argue with laughing until your neck muscles actually ache the next day? If we go through life always taking care of our obligations and make no time to just head out for fun, then life will not be fun, it will be just a series of obligations. Yuk.

CHAPTER 3 – ACTION

I must say that my husband is fun, too. When things were at their worst, he planned a surprise, out of town birthday party for me and it was one of the most uplifting times of my life. Family and friends there just for me. There is not a better feeling! It was a true gift!

In addition to family and friends, I personally feel that giving something of yourself to your community is of utmost importance. Volunteering to help always brings such deep contentment. There is a force in helping others that is difficult to explain but it can be felt by everyone involved – not only those being helped, but also by those helping. Everyone should take time to volunteer!

Sharing joy with those you love and who love you strengthens you. There is power in helping others and letting them help you. I had spent a good deal of time being the helper. I wasn't used to being the one who needed the help. It's good to learn how to let others help you. That is what relationships are all about. That's why they are so important.

Work

What's work doing in a section on taking care of yourself and improving your well-being? It's one of the ingredients? Most people look at work as something they have to do to make money. It is but maybe there is another angle. I think there is. I believe that having meaningful work that you enjoy and feel competent doing is very important to your overall sense of selfworth. Most of us spend a lot of time, over the years, working. We gain skills and have accomplishments. We make decisions and exercise authority. All of this gives us a feeling of control. We get feedback on our performance and from that we develop and mature. When our abilities are challenged and we are able to perform at our optimum level, it gives us a sense of mastery, of "Hey, I'm good at this." I've said it time and time again, I felt so very grateful to have my business during our time of chaos. The satisfaction I gained from starting and growing my business was very important to my mental health. Getting paid for all my hard work and being able to contribute that to the family helped, too.

Nutrition

Okay, now I'm moving into the body stuff. I've pretty much covered the spiritual, soulful, mental aspects, which I personally believe need to be firmly intact before you can really care for your body the way you should. So

CHAPTER 3 – ACTION

now on to the more obvious aspect of caring for ourselves – diet. I mean nutritionally what we eat each day – not the more popular form – what we shouldn't eat. Food is a good thing. It fuels our bodies so we can think straight and perform well. It protects us from disease and can help us heal. We need to eat nutrient-rich foods and make sure we drink enough water. How many times have you heard that? It's more scientific than psychological. Our bodies are like engines, they need to be fueled with high test to perform at peak efficiency. Who today doesn't want to run at peak? We're all trying to do too much so we need an abundance of energy to keep up! Because so many people struggle with being overweight in our culture, food has been given a negative connotation. There seems to be more focus on restriction and deprivation than on nourishment. Why not positive eating – what's good for you rather than what's not – like the National Institutes of Health and other leading health organizations now endorse?

Good nutrition was practiced in my family as I grew up so I understand its value and have reaped the rewards for many (many) years. My mother researched and practiced low-fat, low-cholesterol cooking before it was popular because my father was at high risk for heart disease. As an adult, cooking healthfully is one of my favorite hobbies. I love to cook. It is therapeutic for me to prepare healthful, tasty meals for my family. I am fortunate that I have been able to learn good cooking skills. Good nutrition has definitely made a difference in how I feel and how I look and how I perform. I cannot imagine how much worse I might have felt during our toughest times dealing with Ricky, and all of the rest of the stress in our lives, if I didn't practice good nutrition! Good nutrition has definitely helped Ricky. Because of his neurological imbalances and medication-induced lack of appetite, it is of utmost importance that I understand his nutritional needs and supply healthy food at the right times. I give him his breakfast before his medication in the morning. He eats fruit as soon as he comes home from school before he loses his appetite after taking his medication. I make sure he's hungry for dinner and then feed him a balanced meal. I have to watch him because he craves carbohydrates. I've heard them referred to as "brain food." It seems to make sense that Ricky would crave brain food, BUT I have to watch him and make sure he gets enough other nutrients, too.

CHAPTER 3 – ACTION

Eating healthfully has helped all of us. We are all of average height and weight for our age – except Ricky, he's very thin. Rick and I probably look like we are thin to most people, but we have never "dieted" in the sense of restricting food to lose weight. We all exercise too…I'll get to that next.

I wish people really understood the benefits of proper nutrition. I probably sound naive but I really feel that if folks knew just how empty and nutrient-lacking certain foods are and how damaging they are to their health, they probably wouldn't eat them. I know it is not that simple. Nothing is – but I believe that if people were more educated about good nutrition they would find that it's not difficult to eat healthfully. You don't have to deprive yourself of food to maintain a healthy weight. You need to be aware of eating the right foods at the right time and of drinking enough water.

Rick calls me a "wateraholic." I am, and I'm proud of it. I was drinking loads of water before I even knew how good it was for me. The necessity of water to your health is another thing I'm not sure enough people really understand. Water makes up over half of the weight of our bodies. It's the number one ingredient! We need water to regulate all of our systems. Often dehydration is confused with hunger. Headaches are frequently a sign of dehydration. I know we all hear, "Drink eight ounces of water at least eight times a day," but how many people really do it? I do, and I can tell you if you're active you need even more than that. Please try it. It's another simple thing that makes a huge difference in the way you feel and is paramount to staying healthy. And, an aside, for me I think it even helps my complexion stay a little more on the youthful side. I might not be chronologically youthful but my skin quality is pretty good and I think it's the water!

Back to healthy foods – I'm not a nutritionist and information abounds these days on what's good for you so I'm not going to try to tell you…but, I do have a few tips – I can't resist! Please eat lots of fruits, vegetables, whole grains, and beans. Stay away from highly processed foods – especially sugary foods – they do nothing for your long-term health and are heavy in empty calories. Also, try not to overdo it with drinking alcohol. I like beer. I also think a nice glass of wine with a good meal can't be beat, but too much of anything isn't good. Try eating smaller meals more often rather than three big ones and start with breakfast! Never skip breakfast!

It helps keep your metabolism stable so you have more energy and concentration. Take supplements – you need to figure out which ones you need based on how you eat, but look into antioxidants. They are very important to maintaining good health, especially if you are active. We women need to get enough calcium – drink nonfat milk – you can get used to it – and eat nonfat yogurt. Try to eat a wide variety of foods – the National Cancer Institute says you'll be less likely to die prematurely than those who eat the same few foods day in and day out – plus it's more fun! Substitute the excellent low-fat or fat-free products that are on the market for the regular. Fat-free mayonnaise and low fat cheese cut out a lot of unnecessary fat and calories without compromising flavor. Try the magazine <u>Cooking Light</u>. I love it! It features great variety and it teaches you all you need to know about good nutrition and also about leading a healthy lifestyle. All the recipes I have ever tried have been excellent! Bon Appetit!

Exercise

My favorite! I feel good about the fact that I have been an athlete for most of my life. I swam competitively from the age of five to eighteen, life guarded, coached swimming (and swam) for another four years after that, taught aerobics for four years after that, began running when I met Rick at age twenty-four, and have been running ever since – over twenty years! Additionally, I have professionally provided marketing communication consultation to one of the leading fitness centers in my area. I do not list all of this to sound boastful – ok, maybe I am just a little proud. I list it to lend credibility to what I have to say about the wonders of exercise – because along with good nutrition, regular exercise contributes more to your health than anything else you can do!

I've already told you that for me exercise is essential to my mental fitness. When I wasn't able to work out as I wanted to and needed to, to feel good and relieve stress, it really took its toll mentally. It probably contributed to the decline in my immune system, too. When I moved exercise back up on my priority list, it made a big difference both because of what exercise does physiologically and also because I felt like I was more in control of my time. I was in control enough to do something I wanted and needed to do – and enjoyed doing. Besides, I will be honest, exercise is tied to my self-image. I look better when I exercise. My weight is stable, my skin glows, I

CHAPTER 3 – ACTION

feel stronger and that translates into my personality at meetings and in performing my work – heck, talk about stamina in those long, monotonous meetings! I can last and last and last and with much better sharpness! Whenever possible before a big morning meeting, I work out before I go and I know it improves my performance. And talk about needing extra energy to manage Ricky…I really do honestly thank God that I am physically able to exercise!

Now if that testimonial isn't enough for you, I thought I'd just list a few of the other benefits researchers have found that you can derive from regular exercise: it extends life; helps prevent heart disease, cancer, diabetes, arthritis, and may protect against Alzheimer's; reduces cholesterol levels; reduces blood pressure; strengthens your heart and bones; counters PMS symptoms; deepens sleep; improves hearing; reduces back pain; and cuts sick days in half so you need to see your doctor less! Please, who doesn't want all that?

I think exercise is a gift! So many see it as punishment. If you are physically able and you find an activity that you truly enjoy and then accomplish the feat of carving out the time from your busy schedule to do it and then you reap all of the benefits listed above, isn't that a gift? It's a reward for your body, your mind, and your soul!

I know I can list at least twenty-five excuses for not exercising right now without even stopping to think. I've been around promoting exercise for a long time. All I can say is stop making the excuses and try something. Walk – all you have to do is walk. Once you start and get stronger at any activity you choose, it's contagious. The more you exercise, the better you feel. The better you feel, the more you want to continue. As you set a goal and obtain it, you feel accomplished and proud. You can do it. It all comes back to YOU! You are important. You take care of so many people and things in life. Don't you believe that you deserve to take care of yourself? Exercise is the best place to start. It will immediately make you feel better about yourself, give you increased energy, and then the good cycle begins!

Even though I've been a lifelong exerciser and have trained myself to be "in shape," I still set an annual goal of running a couple of ten-mile races and one half-marathon. I've been doing this for years. The unbelievable feeling of achievement and vitality I feel when I complete

CHAPTER 3 – ACTION

these races is the reason I continue to train. No, I am nowhere near the winner. Just the satisfaction of finishing is enough for me. It's my mind telling my body "you can do it," and my conditioned body rising to the occasion. I get both a mental and a physical lift from the accomplishment! Running these races helps with my everyday training runs. It gives me a goal. Rick trains, too, and then we run the races together. We're usually joined by a few of our running buddies – friends we've met over the years who share our love of running. They are good people. We make a fun time out of these annual events. You can, too. Choose your activity and get out there. The people you meet through exercise share the same value set and it really doesn't get any better than that!

Rest

As loud as I shout about the need to get moving and exercise, at the opposite end of the spectrum, I've become very vocal about the need for rest.

When I was at my most frantic point – trying to get all the help I could for Ricky, start up my business – I was absolutely not getting any rest, and I definitely was not getting enough sleep at night. Bad move. We all need down time and the proper amount of restorative sleep. It is widely known that lack of sleep suppresses the immune system and makes you more susceptible to colds and disease. I also feel it suppresses your whole inner driver, your "can do" mechanism. When you are tired, everything seems like such an uphill battle.

I knew I wasn't getting any down time. I have already written about my need to slow down and the many ways that I accomplished that. It took longer for me to realize I wasn't getting enough sleep. I need more sleep than a lot of people. The experts recommend eight hours per night. I need at least eight and, ideally nine. That's a lot of time! I had so many nightly routines to tend. Once the whole dinner process was done, there was family time and time to look after Ricky's needs, time to iron clothes for the next day, and, I hate to admit it, but during the start-up years of my business, time to actually work in my office at night. I just had to get it all done. You know what I'm talking about!

Racing to do everything we think we need to do when we think we need to do it not only makes each day less enjoyable but from all of the reports I've read lately, it's been cutting into our sleep time and it's wreaking

CHAPTER 3 – ACTION

havoc with everything from our health to our productivity on the job. The key word here is <u>think</u>. If we shift from doing all we think we need to do, to doing just what is necessary at a certain point in time, we'll find that there is time for the proper amount of rest and sleep that is needed to live healthfully and feel good. Again, it's all in how you manage your time and prioritize what's important!

I consciously shifted gears at night. I took everything off my list of things to do after dinner that did not absolutely have to be done and started to focus on winding down, relaxing and reading before bed and then actually turning out the lights an hour earlier. It is amazing how much less Tylenol I have to take and how much less frequent my colds are. I'm not kidding. I think my chronic headaches were not only stress-induced but also a sign of exhaustion. I was ignoring my body's plea for rest! I now know that when my body starts to "hum" (you know that feeling of total fatigue) that that is what it is – fatigue – and not just another headache!

It's remarkable how if you slow down and listen to your body, it will tell you what to do. It really will. Eat when you are hungry, drink water when you are thirsty – actually before, and rest when your body starts to hum!

I now firmly believe in the "power nap." When I need it, just fifteen to twenty minutes of down time restores my energy, clears the way for increased creativity and problem solving and, nine times out of ten, cures even the nastiest head-banging headache! I'm all for the nap rooms that some enlightened companies have established for workers. I think workers need to shift focus from feeling guilty about needing rest to standing up for what their bodies need. Go ahead and tune out for a brief respite from the rushes of the day. It's another gift you can give yourself and you will be pleasantly surprised by the results. Like exercise and good nutrition, rest is nourishment for your mind, body and soul!

I recently read a great article in the Wall Street Journal that defined sleep as the new status symbol. It talked about how the workaholic, overachievers of the 1980s are being replaced by today's truly successful – those who get their eight hours a night. Amen!

Let the Good Cycle Begin!

I know all of this sounds like a lot to do to be healthy and whole. It is. But you are worth it. Making yourself central and taking care of yourself is like the

CHAPTER 3 – ACTION

starter to an engine, it enables the good cycle to begin. And it is a cycle, totally united from beginning to end. The mind, body, and soul are connected and they all work off of one another.

I purposely presented my seven ingredients in a specific order because for me, I needed to quiet my soul – with help from my spiritual beliefs, mental exercises, my relationships and work – before I could move on. Once I had stilled my mind, I could focus on taking care of my body the way I wanted to – and needed to – through good nutrition, exercise and rest.

It doesn't matter where you start. Maybe you need to get your body fueled properly so you can begin to exercise which helps both the body and the mind. Once you are feeling better physically you will feel better mentally and this gives you the motivation and good inner self-talk to continue to eat right, exercise, rest…and the good cycle continues.

I know too many people who just do not start and then they feel guilty. They have a sense of what they could do to live more healthfully and they do not do it. So in addition to not treating themselves as well as they could, they feel guilt on top of it because they know they are not doing what they could to improve their situation. That's a negative cycle if I ever saw one. You're number one. What's good about you? Now believe it and the rest will flow from there!

I am so lucky that I was able to hear myself through the chaos. I'm proud of the way I took care of myself and slowed down and balanced things out. It didn't just help me to physically feel so much better – my colds, headaches and sinus infections basically ceased – but it also helped me to find real joy in life.

As I literally calmed down, I was able to make better decisions about what was best for Ricky and those decisions helped him to progress, too – even his health improved. I could "hear" him so much better. Since I wasn't so overwhelmed, I could be more patient with him. Going with the flow came so much more naturally. I was genuinely ready to accept the messages and our reality more completely. Acceptance became the next step on my path to living wholly.

Acceptance

CHAPTER 4 – ACCEPTANCE

There is a big difference between being aware of something and of accepting something. I had my eyes open and was keenly aware of Ricky's neurological problems. I really understood his situation. I worked very hard to do what was best to help him. I had to go through each of these stages – struggling, understanding, and action – one after the other, but it wasn't until I took the time to slow down and treat myself healthfully that I was ultimately able to receive the most empowering message of all – acceptance. It's empowering because acceptance gives you freedom – freedom from trying to control or change what life has put before you and then it releases you from the anxiety that goes along with living that way. Acceptance allows you to not only live with the struggle but also to grow from it.

I distinctly remember the day I finally said to myself, "So what if Ricky doesn't fit the mold?" And I meant it! I really did! It has made a positive difference in the way I have handled his struggles from that day on. Instead of trying to shape Ricky to be something he was not born to be, I began to celebrate Ricky for being Ricky. I could not have done it without understanding him and working with him to know his strengths and weaknesses.

CHAPTER 4 – ACCEPTANCE

I began to look at Ricky as Ricky and not Ricky as compared to others. Why do we even have to think in terms of "the mold" or "the norm?" Comparisons can be damaging. Better than, best of all, not as good as…we all do it. It's a way to measure one against the other but what do we really accomplish? We either prop ourselves up or bring ourselves down – neither of which is very healthy. Why not just accept and appreciate one another without judging? All of us! I know how hard it is, but Ricky has taught me how and to me, acceptance is the key that opens the door to living wholly.

Honest acceptance finally came to me after one of our many conferences at Ricky's school. Although he was making slow but steady academic progress, we (teacher, administrators and parents) were going over and over Ricky's socialization issues. The teacher was worried that he didn't have any real friendships, that he didn't have good eye contact, that it was like he often had blinders on. They suggested we get him a pet, we enroll him in drama lessons – since he pretended so much – that we sign him up for therapeutic horseback riding lessons. I noted all of this and then Rick and I left to go back to work. As usual, I cried and began to

CHAPTER 4 – ACCEPTANCE

agonize over what should be done. Then it came to me. BOOM! It was absolutely clear. I was not denying that Ricky had socialization issues. BUT…he could relate to others and did. He didn't have any real friendships but he was friendly and kind. He was liked and not bullied. He didn't ostracize himself from anyone because of uncontrollable behavior problems. For a child who struggled with the neurological problems that he did, I'd call that pretty darn good socialization! Ricky had come so far. He wasn't on the playground talking to the sky anymore. Okay, so he did not have a real friend but at least he could be friendly! I thought to myself, "Even in a school for children with substantial learning problems, we're still trying to make him fit the mold. Well, he doesn't fit the mold and he probably never will! He is Ricky and he is doing the best he can! We love him as he is and our acceptance of him has got to be more important to him than getting him a damn dog!" Our acceptance and our pride in <u>his</u> progress in <u>his</u> time!

It took months of one-on-one music therapy, with Ricky and the therapist painstakingly handling and going over each huge vinyl-cut letter while singing the ABC song, to finally "get" the alphabet. But he got it.

CHAPTER 4 – ACCEPTANCE

Then it took many, many more months of a special small group "Reading Mastery" program for him to learn to read. But he can read. He is even the youngest lay reader in our church! It took several years of fine motor therapy for him to be able to hold a pencil and write his name. But he can write and he can even navigate a computer mouse! This from a child who used to start at the bottom left corner of the paper and write diagonally up and across the page, never able to fit what he was trying to write on the page. His letters were huge and hard to read. Once he finally started to get the concept of lines, he would start a sentence in the middle of a line and finish what would not fit above rather than below that line!

Although he still gets special assistance every day to learn the math skills that most children mastered some time ago, he can add and subtract, and multiply and divide! He's starting to get fractions! He's able to participate in gym class now without special assistance. He tells me the other children cheer when he accomplishes something like shooting a basket or blocking a goal! It's taken seven years, but he finally passed the national President's Physical Fitness Test! Success! Definite progress!

CHAPTER 4 – ACCEPTANCE

Ricky just received his first written progress report ever. All of his other prior reports came verbally during school conferences. It has taken years to get close to grade level in most academic areas but he is there! The report was awesome! It has been much, much harder than it is for most children. But he is making unbelievable progress! What more could a mother and father possibly want? For it to be easier? For it to go away and "be all better?" Of course we have felt that way! Sure this has taken every ounce of determination on all of our parts and it has been very hard work and it has been painful and it has taken extreme discipline and much sacrifice. But it is what it is and we're doing the best that we can. Ricky is an extraordinary human being! He is so very loved. We can see his miraculous accomplishments and it inspires us to carry on.

Acceptance shifts your focus from what is not working to what is working. It doesn't mean you give up on the problem areas, it just means you don't dwell on them. You recognize the challenges, but you celebrate the gifts so much more deeply. Ricky has so many gifts. He has an incredible spirit. He can look on the bright side of life and he does! He's kind and intelligent. When

CHAPTER 4 – ACCEPTANCE

he speaks to someone for the first time, they invariably look at me like he's some kind of child prodigy. He is very polite. He's creative – same keen imagination at work since he was a toddler – and he works so hard. He's enthusiastic about life. He's a good swimmer and swims on a summer swim team. He's a good runner. He's a member of the Run Club at school. He has been involved in jujitsu, a grappling form of karate, since he was five years old. First he needed one-on-one lessons, but he's been in a regular class for some time hanging right in there with the rest of them. Obviously his motor skills have improved so much! Things are coming together in Ricky's time.

He knows world affairs better than most adults. He's the only twelve year old – yes twelve, it has taken me some time to finish this book – I know who has his own radio station complete with his own custom-designed logo, microphones, recorders, station jingles, and real interviews of local newsmakers and commentary that rivals Rush Limbaugh. He does it all himself electronically (don't even ask me about the mass of tangled wires – somehow it works – just like his precious tangled brain!) He's even been a guest host on a real

CHAPTER 4 – ACCEPTANCE

local radio talk show on a day off from school. He was composed and knowledgeable. The adult host picked up on that when he first met Ricky and thought it would be interesting to have Ricky on the show to give a youthful perspective. People listened, people called in. The school announced it and other children listened and called in. He knows the news. He loves the news. He asked for (and received) a subscription to <u>Newsweek</u> for Christmas at age eleven. He knows politics. He knows weather. He understands religion. He knows history. He's a whiz on his computer. He understands marketing and advertising. He understands people. He really does know what's going on!

This is a child who went from being physically hunched over, sick, and defeated to a child who understands and accepts himself and accepts life. He is physically healthy. He has not missed a day of school in almost four straight years! I hear him kindly tell people time and time again "That's life!" when he hears them lament about life's seeming unfairness. This is a child who went from total, hysterical frustration over simply changing his navy blue sweater to a child who can make a joke about the impossibility of counting pennies, nickels,

CHAPTER 4 – ACCEPTANCE

dimes and quarters – "I wish we still did it with beans, at least they were all the same color and they were all worth one." This is a child who went from being unable to even throw a ball around with his father to one who beats the pants off of his Dad, fair and square, in Nintendo and XBOX video football and basketball games. He now asks Rick to go outside and shoot real baskets on the court we've had in front of our house since before he was born. He can dribble and shoot – and he likes it! He can even tread water long enough to play a game of water basketball in the deep end of the pool in our backyard.

He knows he's different and he knows he struggles. He understands his neurological impairments. He knows no one is perfect and he knows we all struggle with something – some just more obviously than others. He's the one who reminds me that "I'm okay with myself." He tells me this every time I decide I have to worry about the importance of socialization and playing with friends. Although he has made a friend at school in the years since we were so hung up on "no friendships," he does not have any playmates at home. He does not play regularly outside of school with his one friend. But we are thankful for his friend and his friend's

CHAPTER 4 – ACCEPTANCE

family is thankful for Ricky. Ricky understands his friend. His friend struggles with his motor skills like Ricky used to struggle. Ricky is very tolerant when things get tough for his friend. Ricky has empathy – a trait I am very proud he is able to possess. He gets along with his peers at school and at his summer day camp. He's kind, and even children recognize and respond to that. His social skills are actually more advanced, in many ways, than most children his age, he just doesn't have any regular same-age playmates. He is with Rick and me most all of the time. It used to bother me more than it ever bothered Ricky. He is able to creatively satisfy and occupy himself without the need for playmates. I have noticed an increase in phone calls and Instant Messaging with peers from school. He really is okay with himself! I have faith that the friendships will develop…in Ricky's time.

Ricky has so much potential. He so deserves to be able to realize his potential. He has learned so much. He has done things I honestly didn't think he would ever be able to do. He still struggles. He's still a very challenging child to parent. Rick and I are less at odds with each other over parenting Ricky. It's now more, "we're in this

CHAPTER 4 – ACCEPTANCE

together and it is tough going." It takes an enormous amount of energy to keep up with Ricky because on the one hand he's extremely bright but on the other, he still has considerable trouble with learning and with change. He still needs the individualized attention and small classes at The Pilot School – he's in his eighth year there now. He still needs occupational therapy, only now school offers it so he receives it there. He still loses control – just not as often and not as intensely. It's very hard for him to organize his personal space, but at least he can clean up his room given a lot of time and a lot of patience. He still must be medicated on a daily basis. It's still really hard for him to tie his shoes and get the sheets and blanket and comforter pulled up on his bed anywhere near straight. There are nervous twitches and tics and squeaks that emanate from him at times that are weird and troublesome. I massage him and help him with deep breathing exercises. The same things that help calm me, calm him. We understand these episodes and we accept them. We try really hard not to dwell on them, and when things settle down they go away. They are especially prevalent at the beginning and the end of the school year – his biggest transition times of all. Things

CHAPTER 4 – ACCEPTANCE

are still difficult when he is not on his medication. He chants nonsense in the mornings – like a possessed child – and clothes are still a big strain. I still lose my patience, just not as often. Instead of freaking out, I just stuff the old cotton balls in my ears so I don't have to hear the insanity and then I don't get as frustrated. But, there is a real rhythm to all of this. If I wasn't "well with myself" I would not be able to be in tune to this rhythm. I would still be trying to change it, make it better, or make it go away. Acceptance has empowered me to go with Ricky's flow and it has, by all means, been the catalyst for our growth. It really doesn't feel like we're endlessly paddling upstream anymore. It feels like we're headed in the right direction.

Living Wholly

CHAPTER 5 – LIVING WHOLLY

How do I know that we are headed in the right direction? Because as Ricky's life has unfolded and I've been able to go with it and grow from it, I've realized that it's all been part of the Big Plan. I was supposed to have Ricky. He was meant to be my only child so I could help him and learn from him – a concentrated lesson! I don't know why he was born the way he was but it doesn't matter now. I would never be the person that I am and would never have learned all that I have from his struggles – and mine – if he hadn't been just the way he is. Life is very good and I am very happy. I am not afraid of what will become of Ricky, that's all gone. I know things will be okay, whatever okay is. It may not be what I had dreamed of when I carried him in my womb, maybe it will be even better. We're not there yet and besides, who really ever knows? I have been blessed with this life lesson in wholeness and I believe I was meant to share it. For many years I have enjoyed helping businesses grow, now I'd also like to help people grow. It seems to me, that's heading in the right direction!

I'll try my best to summarize my life lesson in wholeness. It won't be complete because I'm still living it and learning more each day. Ricky will be able to stay at The

Pilot School until he must "mainstream," we pray, into a high school as a freshman – we figure that's about two and a half years from now. In the meantime, here goes…

I have learned that in order to live wholly you must first struggle with something along the way. There are lessons that I have learned that I could never have genuinely understood without struggling. Struggling taught me patience and perseverance – to let it all unfold. I learned that life often does not offer a quick fix, there might be no easy way…but that same truth is what gives life such depth.

In order to persevere, I believe it is imperative to be of sound mind, body and soul. Living wholly is a choice that must come from inside of you and one that takes considerable discipline. But struggling, patience, perseverance, and discipline all pave the way to wisdom, grace, tolerance, compassion, and thankfulness. These are the whole-life gifts that transform you.

<u>Wisdom</u> gives you strength. I am wise. I can say this about myself now even though it's still not easy to say, aloud or to my internal self, such words of praise – but I am wise. And it is because I have struggled. It takes time, but if you don't let your struggle get the best of

you and, instead, you learn from it – understand it, act on it and accept it – you do grow into wisdom.

I think I am wise because I know what is most important in life. It's not the job I have or the job my husband has or the money we earn or the house in which we live or the child with a stellar academic record. It is my commitment to my family and my faith. It is my commitment to helping Ricky and to keeping my marriage healthy and strong. I learned that I cannot change my husband's perception of Ricky's problems or his way of coping. I now understand it is his way and it is different from mine. That's okay. We've grown closer. We're more of a team now.

I am also wise because I have learned the importance of balance. I work hard at being Ricky's advocate. I try to be a good wife. I work hard at running my business and our household…I enjoy working, but I also enjoy my workouts, my "time outs" and my time to be with our families and our friends. I get the same amount of gratification from planning my Sunday School lesson as I do from planning a professional promotional campaign. I used to feel like I should teach Sunday School and the planning was kind of an imposition on my "work" time.

Not anymore! Balance is just that. It is making time for all of the things that are important. And I have learned that it's not just the time but also the presence to thoroughly give to and benefit from whatever you choose to do with your time. You'll know balance when you reach it. You can feel it. It's the flow I've been talking about. It's the opposite of the big rush, the being tugged here and there. It's making a choice about what you do with your time and with your life. It's putting your priorities in order and living them! Wisdom's strength gives you the confidence and courage to balance things out – to do the right thing.

<u>Grace</u> comes to you from doing the right thing. We're culturally so focused on immediate gratification and the quick-fix that it's often hard to do the right thing, especially if the right thing is difficult and requires sacrifice that will cause hardship over a period of time. But doing the right thing is the only way to go. You can never go wrong. Rick and I have done the right thing for Ricky. We have faced his problems head on with all of the resources we have. We have struggled – mentally, physically, emotionally and financially – to do the right thing. But, what a glorious feeling to persevere and then see the growth!

CHAPTER 5 – LIVING WHOLLY

I suggest you learn to truly look at yourself in the mirror and ask yourself if you are doing the right thing – no matter how hard it might be. Are you? Or are you making excuses and believing them and living them? If you look at yourself very closely and with total honesty, you will know the answer. Whom are you hurting if you don't do the right thing? Only yourself, because sooner or later you'll have to face it – and the guilt, because YOU KNOW! Try doing the right thing, right from the start. Grace will be your gift. It really is "Amazing" – just like the hymn says!

<u>Tolerance</u> helps you rise above prejudice. It makes you a better person. We are all different. We really are! Because of Ricky's struggles, I know it now like never before! It has become a mantra for me and for Ricky. Comparisons are harmful so let's all just try very hard to stop. Who are we to judge? I mean it when I say, "Walk a mile in my shoes!" Nobody knows the magnitude of my struggle but me. What right do we have to draw conclusions about others if we don't live their lives? None! Every individual has worth. I have met children through Ricky's school and his various therapies who seem like such negative forces. If you don't

know the child, then you don't understand and you shouldn't judge. Just because a child looks "normal" doesn't mean there isn't something major going on. The same thing goes for all people.

I'm very fond of the 1988 movie "Rain Man" starring Dustin Hoffman. On a certain level it parallels our life with Ricky. Ricky even found the similarities and it made us chuckle. Today at special appearances, the real-life "Rain Man," Kim Peek, who has an astronomical memory but struggles to even bathe and dress himself, ends his presentations by reciting the words that are written on his business card: "Learning to recognize and to respect differences in others and treating them like you want them to treat you will bring the peace and joy we all hope for." Please try to live these words and share them with others.

<u>Compassion</u> takes you out of yourself. It wasn't until I struggled with Ricky that I knew what true, deep compassion for others was like. I worry about the children I've met along the way whose parents do not have access to the resources I am so fortunate to have. Some are misunderstood. Some don't seem to have anyone who really cares. I pray for them and hope that maybe this book will help some of them in some way.

CHAPTER 5 – LIVING WHOLLY

Many days I cried when I stepped inside the children's hospital, where Ricky had years of occupational therapy, and saw pediatric cancer patients. It touched me deep in my heart to see other children in leg braces and wheelchairs waiting with us for therapy. Should it take seeing those children, who with their families know more struggle than we ever will, to remind me how very blessed we are? It shouldn't – but it does. Compassion – it runs very deep.

<u>Thankfulness</u> changes everything. We are each blessed with so many gifts. All we have to do is focus on them. If you're not used to it, it's very easy to begin. Start by being thankful that you wake in the morning able to breathe and move and have independence and the ability to make choices. Yes, take it all the way back to the basics that we take so much for granted. Then don't take them for granted because "the basics" are gifts! As I mentioned early on, if you are the parent of a normal learner or of a child who has natural athletic ability – or you were given these skills yourself – please stop for a moment and recognize them as the gifts that they are!

No one is perfect. We all have strengths and weaknesses – how much time do you spend dwelling on your weaknesses at the expense of celebrating your gifts? Be thankful for all you do have. When you make a point of looking, you'll see there is so much!

I have been given these whole-life gifts of wisdom, grace, tolerance, compassion, and thankfulness. They have directed a bright light into my heart that has opened me up and slowed me down so that I could receive the fullness that life has to offer. My "flow" is totally connected. I am living a balanced life. I cherish every day I live and breathe because I know that life is not a dress rehearsal – it's real, it's now and, I do not know how much of it I have been given or what might be around the next bend on my path. I have done what my heart told me to do – I have written this book. Even though it has taken almost four years to complete this project, I have known all along that it was right and that I could do it. I have gone with my flow. I have balanced my priorities. I now know that you can't go wrong if you live from your heart and have faith to trust the Spirit to guide you.

I am healthy and whole and so is Ricky. I have been blessed with the ability to understand and grow from Ricky's struggles. You've read about how Ricky has grown. I have been given the ability to recall what I have

CHAPTER 5 – LIVING WHOLLY

learned and capture it to share with others so they might grow. I went from having my soul so close to breaking to having my soul sing. I want to help others make that kind of transformation! Life can be so full. Life is meant for living – joyfully living – now, not at some point in the future when you hope your dreams come together or when you think your struggles will be over.

The blossom on the cover glows as an icon of the promise of growth. When Ricky was at his lowest point, he was physically hunched over. He was externalizing how he felt internally. He was mentally and physically withered and so was I. But with **understanding** – like good fertilized soil, **sound actions** based on understanding – like essential water, and **total acceptance** – like the sunlight that makes growth possible, we blossomed and so can you!

Go back now and look at the front cover. Study the blossom. You can see all of the elements radiating growth. Hold the blossom in the eye of your mind and say aloud to yourself, "It's not what life throws at you…it's how you catch it!"

AFTERWORD

Let Someone Know You Care…

I believe that you should try to give more than you receive. I hope that this book has "given" you something. If it has, please share it with someone who could use a little hope and inspiration. You will find that this small act of kindness will mean so much.

In addition, if you have the time, I have always found that if I share lemon sherbet (when it's hot out) or sticky buns (when it's cold out) with someone who needs a lift, it really brightens their day! Both recipes taste great and both are very easy to prepare. They are not low-fat, but "comfort foods" and low-fat don't really go together…anyway, here are my recipes for lemon sherbet and sticky buns. I did not create them, both came from my mother who got the sherbet recipe from the manual that came with her first freezer and the sticky bun recipe has been around.

AFTERWORD

Sticky Buns

Pam Cooking Spray
2 loaves frozen bread dough – thawed (I use Rich's)
1 large box NOT INSTANT vanilla pudding
1 c. brown sugar
1/2 c. (1 stick) margarine
2 tbl. milk
2 tsp. cinnamon
1 c. chopped nuts (I use pecans)
1 c. raisins

Spray 13 x 9 inch pan well with Pam. Sprinkle nuts and raisins in bottom of pan. Pull dough and form into walnut-size balls and make a layer over the nuts and raisins (does not have to be even.) Sprinkle vanilla pudding mix over the dough.

Heat remaining ingredients, mixing well and bring to a boil. Pour over dough balls evenly. Cover tightly with aluminum foil. Store overnight in the refrigerator. Preheat oven to 350. (I take out of the refrigerator & loosen foil about 1/2 hour before baking.) Take foil off and bake for 30 min. Turn onto greased (Pam sprayed) tray so nuts and raisins are on top.

Lemon Sherbet

2 1/2 c. granulated sugar
2/3 c. fresh squeezed lemon juice
grated rind of 2 lemons
4 c. whole milk

Combine sugar, lemon juice and rind. Add milk and stir until sugar is dissolved. Pour into a 13 x 9 inch pan and freeze overnight until firm. Let soften slightly and remove to mixing bowl. Beat until light and creamy and return to freezer (in a plastic container with a tight lid) and allow to finish freezing.

RESOURCES

Excerpt from <u>Sensory Integration and the Child</u> copyright © 1979 by Western Psychological Services. Reprinted by permission of the publisher, Western Psychological Services, 12031 Wilshire Boulevard, Los Angeles, California, 90025, U.S.A. Not to be reprinted in whole or in part for any additional purposes without the expressed, written permission of the publisher. All rights reserved.

Definitions from <u>Understanding Sensory and Motor Challenges in the Classroom</u> booklet copyright © 1993 used with permission of the publisher, Sensory Integration International, P.O. Box 5339, Torrance, California 90510. Phone: (310) 787-8805 www.sensoryint.com

<u>Very helpful program</u>: "How Does Your Engine Run?" A Leader's Guide to the Alert Program for Self-Regulation. Published by TherapyWorks, Inc., 4901 Butte Place N.W., Albuquerque, NM 87120. Phone (505) 897-3478.

continued

RESOURCES

<u>Very helpful therapy products:</u> Pocket Full Of Therapy, P.O. Box 174, Morganville, NJ 07751. Phone (732) 441-0404, (800) PFOT-124, www.pfot.com

Sensory Comfort, P.O. Box 6589, Portsmouth, NH 03802 (888) 436-2622, www.sensorycomfort.com

<u>National Center for Learning Disabilities</u>, 381 Park Avenue South, Suite 1401, New York, NY 10016, (212) 545-7510, (888) 575-7373, www.ncld.org

ORDER FORM

FAX ORDERS: (302) 733-7618. (Please fax this form.)
PHONE ORDERS: (302) 733-7661. (Please have the information on this form ready.)
MAIL ORDERS: NPF Communications, 95 Iroquois Ct., Newark, DE 19702

Please send me the following quantity of Blossom! I understand that if I am not satisfied, I may return the book(s) for a full refund.

QUANTITY	PRICE EACH	PRICE TOTAL
_____ x	$12.95 =	$_____
	TOTAL SHIPPING*	$_____
	* Add $4.00 for the first book & $2.00 for each additional book	
	TOTAL PRICE	$_____

SHIP TO:

Name:_____

Address:_____

City:_____ State:_____ Zip:_____

Phone: (_____) _____ email:_____

PAYMENT: ○ Check (Payable to NPF Communications)   ○ Visa   ○ MasterCard

Credit Card #:_____ Exp. Date:_____

Name As It Appears On Card:_____

Signature:_____

How Did You Hear About *Blossom!?*_____

Please Contact Me About Speaking/Seminars: ○ Yes   ○ No

Questions? Call (302) 733-7661 or check our website: npfcommunications.com

Thank You For Your Order